Literacy As Social Exchange

Intersections of Class, Gender, and Culture

Maureen M. Hourigan

STATE UNIVERSITY OF NEW YORK PRESS

Published by
State University of New York Press, Albany

© 1994 State University of New York

Printed in the United States of America

For information, address State University of New York
Press, State University Plaza, Albany, N.Y., 12246

Production by E. Moore
Marketing by Bernadette LaManna

Library of Congress Cataloging-in-Publication Data
Hourigan, Maureen M., 1942–
    Literacy as social exchange: intersections of class, gender, and
culture/Maureen M. Hourigan.
        p.   cm. — (SUNY series literature, culture, and learning)
    Includes bibliographical references and index.
    ISBN 0–7914–2069–8. — ISBN 0–7914–2070–1 (pbk.)
    1. Literacy—Social aspects—United States.   2. Educational
anthropology—United States.   3. Critical pedagogy—United
States.   4. Multicultural education—United States.   I. Title.
II. Series.
LC151.H68   1994
370.19'2'0973—dc20   93–43234
                                                                    CIP

10 9 8 7 6 5 4 3 2 1

To Jim

Contents

Foreword

At last, scholars are beginning to recognize that literacy is not an isolated "skill" that "individuals" independently "acquire"; rather, it is deeply embedded in and produced by cultural forces and practices. It is, in short, a product of "social exchange." Class, race, ethnicity, and gender all play crucial roles in the production and reception of literate behaviors, as well as in our very notions of what literacy itself is. Thus, any scholarly examination of literacy or writing pedagogy necessarily must account for the complex interplay of social forces. This is exactly what Maureen Hourigan does in this fascinating and important study of the influence of class, gender, and culture on students' learning to negotiate the conventions of academic discourse.

Recent literacy scholarship has tended to isolate gender, class, and race as discrete marginalizing factors; but such isolation, Hourigan argues, may well "unintentionally silence voices from non-Western, non-mainstream cultures." She wisely argues that we must examine how all these cultural factors together influence how students learn to read, write, and think critically if we are going to be able to position ourselves to construct effective writing pedagogies that address the needs of *all* students in our increasingly more multicultural classroom.

This lucid, cogent, beautifully written book (Hourigan's friendly yet authoritative voice is omnipresent) is provocative, raising significant questions, often by employing astonishing factual data. I am particularly drawn, for example, to her discussion in chapter 2 of how some of the most influential scholars writing about "basic writing" (and about the plight of the underprivileged) themselves teach at some of the most elite, exclusive institutions in the nation. A detailed student profile of these institutions reveals that these "under-privileged" basic writers are nowhere near as disadvantaged as many of the students we ourselves encounter every day. As Hourigan explains, "the portrait of basic writing students painted in broad strokes in many journal articles is a portrait of a very specific group of basic writing students housed within the halls of America's most competitive colleges and universities." Thus, the scholarship offers us an unreliable portrait of the "basic" writer, one somewhat out of touch with the daily realities of basic writing instruction in most institutions across the country.

Also revealing is Hourigan's discussion in chapter 4 of "the increasingly diverse multicultural classroom that com-position teachers can expect to face" by the turn of the century. Hourigan skillfully explores enrollment trends in higher education—trends that indicate conclusively that soon our classrooms will be substantially populated by students from non-Western, non-mainstream cultures. These students' rhetorical and literacy traditions will be unlike those both of their teachers and of the "basic writers" we currently hear so much about in the scholarly literature. Consequently, as educators and literacy scholars we will need increasingly to conceptualize literacy in its larger political, social, and economic contexts, to contend with literacy on the less-familiar terrain of class, race, and ethnicity. Such expanded conceptualizing of literacy will better equip us to construct writing pedagogies that are at once efficacious and respon-sive to the diverse needs of our increasingly diverse student populations.

Literacy As Social Exchange: Intersections of Class, Gender, and Culture is an important, provocative, critical examination of the intersection of culture and literacy educa-tion. In its attempt to convince us to focus on the larger picture of how numerous cultural forces together affect literacy, this book helps prepare all of us for the thoroughly multicultural classrooms of the twenty-first century. *Literacy As Social Exchange* is a must for anyone concerned with literacy.

GARY A. OLSON

Introduction

Why is literacy of such interest to
postsecondary teachers of writing? If "literacy,"
as it might be defined by someone outside the
field of English studies, is "the ability to read
and write," then why are we interested in it
when our students presumably acquired this
ability in the distant past, about the time they
learned to tie bows in their shoelaces?
                                    —"Professing"

So begins Patricia Bizzell's review essay of recent
scholarship on issues of literacy relevant to composition
studies. Of course, the lighthearted tone of Bizzell's second
question lets her audience know at the outset that she will
reject such a simple definition of literacy. But her almost
playful juxtaposition of literacy and a child's learning to tie
her shoelaces belies the seriousness of the issues that Bizzell
is addressing, and it is with grim seriousness that she answers
her first question:

> In short, I think we are talking about literacy because we are
> having a collective identity crisis about being English teachers,
> and, in particular, we are very unclear as to what good we are
> doing for the larger society with our efforts. (316)

Literacy has often been identified with a crisis of one sort
or another. Much of the current literacy-as-crisis discourse
can be traced to *Newsweek*'s widely read, highly influential
"Why Johnny Can't Write," published in 1975. Its graphic
displays of "illiterate prose" mobilized educators and poli-

ticians alike to offer explanations for and to propose solutions to a national "literacy crisis" that touched even the
most educationally advantaged students at Harvard and
Yale. Unlike most other media crises, the literacy crisis has
remained a surprising exception to what news editors term
the "Weekend Yawn Rule."[1] In the summer of 1987, a dozen
years after *Newsweek's* cries of dismay, both E. D. Hirsch Jr.'s
Cultural Literacy: What Every American Should Know and
Allan Bloom's *The Closing of the American Mind* received
considerable media attention and remained high on the
national list of best-sellers for several weeks; in fact, more
than 650,000 hardcover copies of Bloom's book were sold
(House, Emmer, and Lawrence 58–59).

Although a comprehensive definition of literacy is
beyond the scope of Bizzell's review essay, a comprehensive
definition of literacy is precisely what is needed in the current discourse where "literacy" has become a catchall term
of many meanings. This study, drawing upon poststructural
theories of language use, argues for a social definition of
literacy. Like Richard Ohmann, I contend that

> it is not helpful to think of literacy as an invariant, individ-
> ual skill. . . . Literacy is an activity of social groups, and a
> necessary feature of some kinds of social organization. Like
> every other human activity or product, it embeds social rela-
> tions within it. And these relations always include *conflict* as
> well as cooperation. Like language itself, literacy is an ex-
> change between classes, races, the sexes, and so on. (*Politics of
> Letters* 226)

More specifically, this study focuses on issues of literacy
as they play themselves out in late twentieth-century postsecondary institutions. Here, the concern is with "critical
literacy," especially as defined in relation to argumentative
discourse. Linda Flower, for one, defines the critically literate
person as one who "questions sources, looks for assumptions,
and reads for intentions, not just facts" and "transforms
[information] for a new purpose" (Flower et al 5). For Mike
Rose, critical literacy involves "framing an argument or taking someone else's argument apart, systematically inspecting

a document, an issue, or an event, synthesizing different points of view, applying a theory to disparate phenomena, and so on" (*Lives* 188). But these "sophisticated literacy activities" now expected of students at all institutions can pose special problems for students marginalized by class, gender, or culture. Rose points out that these are skills to which many underprepared students have had little exposure (*Lives* 188). And Marilyn M. Cooper, who emphasizes argumentative skills in her definition of "academic discourse," describes the difficulties that students, women especially, experience when attempting to negotiate its conventions. She explains that "even after two quarters or semesters of writing instruction, many first-year students still cannot analyze ideas complexly or argue positions logically; in other words, they do not take well or easily to academic discourse" ("Women's" 141).

This study explores the roles that class, gender, and culture play in students' abilities to negotiate the conventions of academic discourse. As such, it extends critiques of class and gender as marginalizing factors, considering the role that culture may play in the difficulties that some students (men and women both) encounter with academic discourse. Throughout, it argues that current critiques, in their isolation of class or gender as marginalizing factors, encourage the adoption of pedagogies that may unintentionally silence voices from non-Western, non-mainstream cultures, and it calls for research that investigates the intersection of these factors.

OVERVIEW OF THE STUDY

In order to avoid what Henry Giroux terms "historical amnesia" (*Schooling* 4) and in order to dispel what Mike Rose calls the "myth of transience"—the belief that "if we can just do x or y, the problem [of illiteracy] will be solved ("Language" 355)—Chapter 1 provides a brief review of literacy crises and campaigns. By comparing the literacy crises of the 1890s with those of the last quarter of the twentieth century and by pointing out the similarities in campaigns designed to wipe out functional illiteracy and those designed to improve students' abilities to negotiate the conventions of academic discourse, I want to emphasize that similar social, political, and economic objectives underpin almost all discussions of literacy, whether defined as functional or academic.

Chapter 2 focuses on basic writing as an important site of the literacy/illiteracy debate, challenging the widely held perception of basic writers as "disempowered lower class students" (Miller 172). Although studies by David Bartholomae, Bizzell, and Rose have offered a much needed corrective to the notion of basic writers as "deficient," I show how these scholars' focus on basic writers who are "outsiders" in competitive colleges and universities presents a limited and limiting portrait of such writers. In addition, this chapter presents a critique of radical pedagogies designed to empower students marginalized by class. I contend that these pedagogies may be counterproductive in less competitive postsecondary institutions, for the practical literacy that so many "middle-class" students seek is often at odds with the critical literacy that their radical writing teachers seek to impart.

The feminist critique of gender as a marginalizing factor in students' abilities to write argumentative discourse provides the focus for Chapter 3. The effects of the social relationships between men and women outside the classroom on the relationships of men and women inside the classroom are of particular interest to compositionists. This chapter examines the influence of feminist studies in the fields of psychology, sociolinguistics, and speech communication on feminist compositionists' studies. While acknowledging that research on gender-specific features and problems with writing has produced a much expanded theory of the composing process and the nature of its finished products, I point out that, in its focus on women only, such research may reinforce cultural myths about gender. Furthermore, I suggest that the open-ended, exploratory, and often autobiographical writing associated with feminist pedagogy is not appropriate for groups marginalized by other factors in their relation to language. More specifically, I point out that a pedagogy centered on autobiographical writing may even silence women marginalized by both class and gender.

Chapter 4 paints a picture of the increasingly diverse multicultural classrooms that composition teachers can expect to face in almost all institutions of higher learning by the year 2000. Because the social, political, and economic concerns that underpin all discussions of language use and instruction become more public when the site of the literacy/illiteracy debate shifts to issues of race and ethnicity, Chapter 4 begins with a brief sketch of the political climate in the United States in the early 1990s, capturing in broad brushstrokes the fears, the anxieties—at times, the desperation—of Americans looking for an answer to what they perceive as a decline in the American quality of life. Against this backdrop, I paint another picture, that of composition classrooms filled with bilingual students, students from foreign countries, students born in the United States who speak a language other than English as their first language. In short, this is a portrait of classrooms of the twenty-first century, classrooms filled with students from non-Western, non-mainstream cultures whose rhetorical traditions and definitions of communicative competence differ not only from their teachers' but also from those students' upon whom so much composition scholarship focuses. In addition, this chapter draws upon studies in contrastive rhetoric and sociolinguistics to explain the differences between Asian rhetoric, in particular, and Western rhetoric. Although Asian rhetoric shares many features with discourse labeled "feminine," this chapter illustrates that important differences in perceptions of communicative competence characterize these discourses as well.

In Chapter 5 I turn from a focus on the isolation of variables in composition studies to a focus on the intersection of disciplines within the field. More specifically, I show that basic writing and feminist pedagogies, as well as those designed to empower students from other cultures, incorporate both reading and writing in their recommendations. In addition, this chapter considers the centrality of the "conversation" metaphor in discussions of reading and writing, suggesting that reading-as-conversation, like social conversations themselves, is a more complex construct than some compositionists have realized. Center stage in this chapter, however, belongs to a "snapshot" of Ms. L, a returning, part-time student in her mid-forties. Employing new methods of research that Elizabeth A. Flynn argues are needed for new research questions ("Composing 'Composing'" 84), I show how Ms. L's personal background shaped her response to an argumentative research paper assignment.

This study concludes with a discussion of the implications for future research and suggestions for meeting the needs of increasingly multicultural classrooms. It calls for studies that consider the intersection of class, gender, and culture and demonstrates the need for ethnographic studies of home literacies. It encourages inhabitants of different compartments within the field of composition to collaborate with one another, and it recommends that compositionists be more open to multiple literacies in their classrooms. Most importantly, it asks compositionists to take every available speaking opportunity to work toward a new public conception of literacy, one that not only acknowledges the value of multiple literacies but also recognizes that literacy "crises" are not solved in a few years with a few prescriptive top-down literacy programs. No specific pedagogy is suggested for the increasingly diverse multicultural classrooms of the future, for good pedagogies must always be local ones, changing from one place to another, from one semester to another, often, indeed, from one classroom to another.

As for postsecondary English teachers' collective identity crisis, Bizzell's re-vision of her role as a writing instructor at Holy Cross might serve as a vision for all of us:

> I no longer see myself as the privileged advocate for marginalized basic writers. . . . I increasingly see my situation as analogous to that of basic writers—what I had thought of as specifically their experience I now see as paradigmatic for all American experience. Another way to put this would be to say that I now see all teachers as more like students, and all students as more like basic writers, than I once did.
>
> (*Academic* 129–30)

1

Literacy Crises and Campaigns in Perspective

[T]o consider any of the ways in which literacy
intersects with social, political, economic,
cultural, or psychological life requires
excursions into other records.
                                    —Harvey J. Graff

"Willy-nilly, the U.S. educational system is spawning a generation of semiliterates" (Sheils 58). With this pronouncement, *Newsweek*'s "Why Johnny Can't Write" created a national panic about the state of functional and cultural literacy in the United States in the 1970s. But in offering statistics that "grow more appalling each year" (58), Merrill Sheils did not mention that definitions of literacy are imprecise and literacy rates scarce. Nor did she acknowledge that literacy crises and preparatory instruction have long been features of American education and that this "scenario has gone on for so long that it might not be temporary" (Rose, "Language" 355).

Unlike Sheils, Carl F. Kaestle and his coeditors point out the inherent difficulties in discussing literacy statistics from a historical perspective. Because definitions of literacy are confusing and imprecise, the data are incomparable over time. All in all, they conclude, "We know very little about the distribution and uses of literacy over the last century" (xiv). The shifting definitions of "functional literacy" provide a case in point. In the 1930s, the Civilian Conservation Corps defined functional literacy as a fourth-grade educational level; by 1947, the Census Bureau considered anyone with fewer than five years of schooling illiterate. Five years later, the standard of functional literacy had risen to a sixth-grade educational level, and by 1960, the U.S. Office of Education defined functional literacy as an eighth-grade educational level (92). In 1973, the "Report of the Committee on Reading, National Academy of Education" concluded that "a meaningful goal [of minimal literacy] would be the attainment of twelfth-grade literacy" (Carroll and Chall 8). Carman St. John Hunter and David Harman likewise note that "in the United States... completion of secondary school has become a kind of benchmark definition of functional literacy" (27). In general, they argue that literacy should be defined as

> The possession of skills *perceived as necessary by particular persons and groups* to fulfill their own self-determined objectives as family and community members, citizens, job-holders, and members of social, religious, or other associations of their choosing. This includes the ability to obtain information they want and to use that information for their own and others' well-being; the ability to read and write adequately to satisfy the requirements *they set for themselves* as being important for their lives; the ability to deal positively with demands made on them by society; and the ability to solve the problems they face in their daily lives. (7–8)

Although this discussion of shifting definitions of literacy illustrates the difficulties of comparing literacy rates historically, a comparison of the origins of literacy crises and campaigns of the last half of the nineteenth century with those of the last quarter of the twentieth century is instructive, for it reveals that similar social, political, and economic features underlie the crises and campaigns of both centuries. In fact, Robert F. Arnove and Harvey J. Graff contend that the initiation of literacy campaigns from the Protestant Reformation to the present "has been associated with major transformations in social structure and belief systems," and that "key common elements"—"mission, organization, pedagogy, and content"—unite them "across time and space" (4, vii). Such has been the case in the United States, as Richard Ohmann points out: "Each time the American educational system has rapidly expanded, admitting previously excluded groups to higher levels, there has been a similar chorus of voices lamenting the decline in standards and foreseeing the end of Western civilization" (*Politics of Letters* 234). Analyzing the American economy in the context of long-term social moods in the country, economist Henry Gailliot draws parallels between the political and social distress brought about by the decline of the agrarian society and the rise of a manufacturing society in the late 1800s and the current political and social stress brought about by an economy where "employment skills and the employment locations do not mesh well with the demand" (6–7). Both periods are representative of the "parochial" phase in the country's "social value cycle," he explains, where divisive issues, often marked by moral overtones and driven by economics, dominate the social mood (4). Thus, the literacy crisis of the last quarter of the twentieth century (the divisiveness of which is detailed in Chapter 4) can be viewed as driven as much by economics as by a concern for students' declining writing abilities. In the words of J. Elspeth Stuckey, the "high profile of literacy" is "symptomatic of a speedy, ruthless transition from an industrial to an information based economy" (viii).

FROM CRISIS TO CAMPAIGN (1840–1910)

From 1800 to 1870, literacy campaigns in the United States were inaugurated in response to growing tensions in an increasingly pluralistic society. By the middle of the nineteenth century, pluralism was regarded as a threat to cultural unity. The polarization of Protestant and Catholic, foreigner and native, strained the belief in an essentially homogeneous and consensus-based social order. The public school offered a mechanism to overcome religious and ethnic diversity and to transcend the emerging tensions in the American social order. (Stevens 117)

Advocates of a public school system ostensibly sought to inculcate "fundamentals of literacy," but the "common elements of American culture" they defined as "fundamentals" amounted to the imposition of the values of the "prominent in society" upon the rest (117).

The cultural diversity that led to the institution of the public school system also led to the growth of the universities from 1870 to 1910. Between 1870 and 1890 alone, student enrollment in the universities increased threefold, from 50,000 to 150,000 students; by 1910, enrollment had more than doubled again (Kerr xii). Laurence R. Veysey speculates that increasing cultural diversity fueled this growth, for it was during these years that numbers of immigrants from "new and less respectable sources" increased. Already-established American immigrants from northern Europe felt the need to distinguish themselves, and a university degree—"impressive, preeminently wholesome, and increasingly accessible to any family affluent enough to spare the earning power of its sons in their late teens"—became one "emphatic trademark" of the social mobility of these northern European immigrants (265–66). Of course, perception of a university education as a hallmark of success was not the only reason higher education expanded. Land-grant universities, specializing in "service to the productive elements of society—especially to agriculture and to industry," proliferated during this time and needed to enroll a whole new population if they were to continue to grow (Kerr xi).

This new population of students led to a perceived decline in students' writing abilities and a spate of *Newsweek*-like reports decrying them. In the 1840s, for example, the president of Brown University railed against incoming students' poor grammatical skills (Rose, *Lives* 5). In 1871, the president of Harvard University, Charles William Eliot, reported:

> The need of some requisition which should secure on the part of young men preparing for college proper attention to their own language has long been felt. Bad spelling, incorrectness as well as inelegance of expression in writing, ignorance of the simplest rules of punctuation, and almost entire want of familiarity with English literature, are far from rare among young men of eighteen otherwise well prepared for college. (qtd. in Daniels 51)

As a consequence of the perception that incoming students' language use was deficient, Harvard instituted entrance examinations for all incoming students whether "sons of the aristocracy or those few poor youths of demonstrated 'capacity and character'" (52). However, the institution of neither placement examinations nor freshman composition seemed to improve much the writing abilities of Harvard's young men. In 1885, Harvard Professor Adams Sherman Hill confessed,

> Every year Harvard graduates a certain number of men—some of them high scholars—whose manuscript would disgrace a boy of twelve; and yet the college cannot be blamed, for she can hardly be expected to conduct an infant school for adults. (qtd. in Daniels 52)

In 1896, *The Nation* published "The Growing Illiteracy of American Boys," wherein the Committee of the Overseers of Harvard College on Composition and Rhetoric placed the blame for its students' growing illiteracy squarely on the shoulders of the preparatory schools. The Committee argued that

> students came up from the leading preparatory schools in such a condition of unfitness, as regards their own tongue, that it was necessary for the college to spend much time, energy and money in teaching them what they ought to have learnt already. (284)

Harvard resented such expenditures as the words of Professor Goodwin make clear: "There was no conceivable justification for using the revenues of Harvard College or the time and strength of her instructors in a vain attempt to enlighten the Egyptian darkness in which no small portion of her undergraduates were sitting" (284). In fact, the angry members of the Committee decided to illustrate their concerns by publishing "deplorable" specimens of entrance examinations written by students of Boston Latin School, Mr. Noble's, and Roxbury Latin.

The principals of Boston Latin School, Mr. Noble's, and Roxbury Latin filed a protest with the Committee, shifting the blame for the growing illiteracy of Harvard's students from their schools to the sad state of literacy in the community at large. In terms that sound arrestingly familiar to twentieth-century ears, they complained:

> While we regret the growing illiteracy of American boys as much as your committee does, we cannot feel that the schools should be held solely responsible for evils which are chiefly due to the absence of literary interest and of literary standards in the community. (284)

Subsequent issues of *The Nation* printed numerous letters in response to the report from Harvard, most sharing the principals' view that a general decline in literacy in society was to blame for the "condition of unfitness" in which so many of the nation's most academically privileged young men found themselves. Responses from Connecticut to California echoed the sentiments of William F. Brewer of Bozeman, Montana, who wrote,

> The time [students] spent in the study of grammar or composition during their earlier schooling, even if well spent, has counted little in comparison with influences elsewhere. The home, the very cheap newspaper, the street have furnished them with their common speech. (327)

Edward G. Coy of Lakeville, Connecticut, concurred, pointing out that trying to teach children the language that Harvard expected of them on examinations "is often as impossible of achievement as would be the effort to make a silk purse out of a pig's ear" (344).

But Elmer L. Curtiss, Superintendent of Schools from Hingham, Massachusetts, found a different reason for the boys' illiteracy, namely, the colleges' failure to respond to their increasingly pluralistic student body. As he explains,

> The lower schools have responded to the needs of the time and have adapted themselves to the social and economic changes, while the high schools are still under the bondage of an educational system centuries old—a system, by the way, that the colleges perpetuate and force upon all schools sending pupils to them. (420–21)

It was just this increasingly pluralistic student body that worried the "California teacher" who wrote to complain about the growth of Berkeley and the relaxation of entrance standards at the University of California. Noting that Berkeley had increased its enrollment fivefold in just ten years and that the University of California had decreed that students from sixty-seven designated secondary schools could enter without having to take entrance examinations, the California teacher wondered in print what such actions might portend. Quoting in part from one of California's university presidents and from Edward, Lord Bulwer-Lytton, he laments,

> "[T]he inevitable result [of] placing every fifty-cent boy or girl within reach of a two-thousand dollar college education" . . . must be to bring about a condition of affairs to which Bulwer-Lytton refers in one of his works with an almost prophetic pathos . . . : "It is not from ignorance henceforth that society will suffer—it is from over-educating the hungry thousands who, thus unfitted for manual toil, and with no career for mental, will puzzle wiser ministers than I am." ("How to Build Up a University" 494–95)

Despite this "California Teacher" 's concerns, the universities continued to expand. Their growth from 1870 to 1910 marked one of the two great transformations in higher education in the United States (Kerr xi). (The other great transformation, which occurred from 1960 to 1980, I will address shortly.)

As universities grew in size and number and as their missions and populations changed, so, too, did the types of writing required of their students. Before 1860 the focus of the American colleges and preparatory schools was spoken language; writing was "merely an aid to memory" (Russell 4). Recitation was the preferred mode of instruction, and students were often required to memorize pages from a text and repeat them back to a teacher (Kitzhaber 2). However, as the American educational system expanded to include public high schools, land-grant universities, and trade schools, private as well as public schools began to view their educational mission in a new light. As James Berlin explains, both began to see themselves as "serving the needs of business and industry. Citizens demanded it, students demanded it, and most important, business leaders—the keepers of the funds—demanded it" (60). Writing, too, changed from oral transcription of speech to texts required of graduates preparing for careers other than the pulpit or the bar. New professions in business and industry required reports, specifications, and memoranda. Although this educational society now saw itself as a training ground for new professionals, David Russell contends that it "failed to adjust its concept of writing for the fact that both writing and education had been transformed," clinging instead to "the outmoded conception of writing as transcribed speech and to the vanishing ideal of a single academic community, united by common values, goals, and standards of discourse" (5).

One of the effects of this failure to adjust the concept of writing was the spate of Harvard Reports (1892, 1895, 1897) decrying the poor writing skills of students at Harvard. Another was Harvard's response: the institution of entrance examinations (whose list of required readings is the forerunner of E. D. Hirsch's) and the institution of freshman composition. Both Albert R. Kitzhaber and Berlin acknowledge the historical importance of Harvard's entrance examinations and freshman composition program. Kitzhaber asserts that Harvard's English program established a pattern for almost all universities (33), and Berlin adds that its focus on superficial error "gave support to the view that has haunted writing classes ever since: learning to write is learning matters of superficial correctness"(62). Furthermore, Berlin contends, after the Harvard Reports, "the mark of an educated man" was his ability to use the dialect of the upper middle class. In order to secure entry into the upper classes, children of the lower classes had to demonstrate their mettle by learning this dialect. Composition teachers became the "caretakers of the English tongue" and the "gatekeepers on the road to the good things in life." Not surprisingly, composition texts of this time were devoted to superficial correctness, that most significant mark of educated prose. In short, Berlin notes, these texts "were designed to serve the professional aspirations of the middle class" (72–73). But for all their influence, neither the Harvard Reports nor the writing programs and texts that they engendered addressed, in Russell's words, the real problems: "Standards of literacy were no longer stable; they were rising, and more importantly, multiplying" (6). Many of these same situations and solutions are mirrored in the current literacy crisis, a crisis that occurred after the second great transformation in American higher education, the period from 1960 to 1980.

FROM CRISIS TO CAMPAIGN (1960–1993)

In 1983, the President's National Commission on Excellence in Education declared that declining test scores and writing skills threatened the nation's security; we had become *A Nation at Risk*. In 1986, in a hearing before the Senate Subcommittee on Elementary, Secondary, and Vocational Education, Senator Edward Zorinsky testified that the "schools are creating illiterates" and that reforms could not be left up to the educators (Stedman and Kaestle 77). On the tenth anniversary of *A Nation at Risk*, *The Chronicle of Higher Education* reported that although "the school reform movement has galvanized business and government, leading to dozens of blue-ribbon panels, widespread state reforms—and a new generation of jargon," "professors on the front lines of undergraduate instruction," like those professors quoted in the "Johnny" articles of the mid-1970s, contend that students "are not familiar with the written word," and "spend too much time in front of the television" (Zook A19, A24).

Ernest R. House, Carol Emmer, and Nancy Lawrence deftly sketch the economic and social climate in which the literacy campaign of the last quarter of the twentieth century is situated:

> The deteriorating economic condition of the United States, the development of a seemingly permanent underclass, and the entry of vast numbers of non-English speaking immigrants, legal and illegal, have created a situation in which many Americans feel threatened. . . . In addition, there is a pervasive sense of unease about the United States' slipping economically, as reflected in rising trade deficits and a stagnant standard of living. All this concern begs for an answer. . . . (72)

Literacy became an answer, in much the same way that literacy had become an answer to the cultural diversity of the period from 1800 to 1870. In its "second great transformation" from 1960 to 1980, just as in the period from 1870 to 1910, enrollments mushroomed, and a new population of students provided much of the growth. By 1980, for example, 12 million students were enrolled in institutions of higher learning, an increase of 8.5 million students in just twenty years. Minorities represented 17 percent of the total enrollment in 1980, an increase of 7 percent from 1960, and women students, by the slimmest of margins, had become the majority (Kerr xiv).[2]

The University of California president who puzzled over the wisdom of admitting "fifty-cent" boys and girls to the universities in 1896 would no doubt have been awestruck at Mina Shaughnessy's description of the students attending City University of New York in 1970:

[I]n the spring of 1970, the City University of New York...
[opened] its doors not only to a larger population of students
than it had ever had before... but to a wider range of students
than any college had probably ever admitted or thought of
admitting to its campus—academic winners and losers from
the best and worst high schools in the country, the children of
the lettered and the illiterate, the blue-collared, the white-
collared, and the unemployed, some who could barely afford
the subway fare to school and a few who came in the new cars
their parents had given them as a reward for staying in New
York to go to college. (1–2)

As the populations of the universities changed, so,
too, did their missions. The percentage of students enrolled
in traditional arts and sciences programs declined, while
the percentage of those enrolled in preprofessional programs
increased. From 1969 to 1976 alone, enrollment in the preprofessional programs grew from 38 to 58 percent. In the
words of Clark Kerr, Chairman of the Carnegie Commission
on Higher Education from 1967 to 1980, "This was the last
and conclusive triumph of the Sophists over the Philosophers,
of the proponents of the commercially useful over the
defenders of the intellectually essential" (xiii).

Writing instruction in the transformed university had a
curious fate. In the 1960s, while higher education tended to
the business of expansion, composition requirements were
either dropped or reduced in one-third of all four-year colleges
and universities (Russell 272). Those courses that were offered
revived personal writing as a means of expressing support
for political movements and challenging authority; political
critique, however, remained largely implicit (Herzberg 111–
12). But by the 1970s, as the expanded higher educational
system brought about increased access, colleges and universities witnessed the "widest social and institutional demand
for writing instruction since mass-education had founded
composition a century earlier to solve the problem of integrat-
ing new students into academia" (Russell 275). With the
arrival of such students as Shaughnessy describes, personal
writing and the development of authentic voice became less

important. The goal of many of the new writing courses developed in the late 1970s and early 1980s was to initiate this new population of students into the conventions of academic discourse.

Shaughnessy's new students and their difficulties with academic discourse no doubt provided much of the impetus for *Newsweek*'s reports of the declining writing abilities of American students and the calls for reforms. But much of the focus was on the writing of students at our most elite universities. "What makes the *new illiteracy* so dismaying," declared *Newsweek*'s Sheils, "is precisely the fact that writing ability among even the best-educated young people seems to have fallen so far so fast" (59; emphasis added). But, as the foregoing discussion has illustrated, the level of writing skills among students in even our most elite universities had been dismaying their educators for more than a century before *Newsweek*'s report. Furthermore, the remarks by Harvard's Hill and Goodwin belie Sheils's claims that the literacy crisis in 1975 was different from that reported one hundred years earlier, for in both instances the crisis focused on the inarticulate expression of students at our most culturally and educationally elite institutions.

Other similarities in the two crises are apparent as well. Like the earlier literacy campaign, colleges and universities sought to place the blame on students' high school preparation and a decline in higher-level literacy activities in a culture influenced by the popular media. Sheils quoted professors who claimed that by the time students reach college, "the breakdown in writing has been in the making for years"; in addition, they cited causes ranging from "inadequate grounding in the basics of syntax, structure and style to the popularity of secondary-school curriculums that no longer require the wide range of reading a student must have to learn to write clearly" (59). High school teachers who "have simply stopped correcting poor grammar and sloppy construction" were singled out for blame by Northwestern's Dr. Elliott Anderson (qtd. in Sheils 60). Just as Mr. Brewer blamed "the very cheap newspaper" for the decline in students' writing abilities in 1896, E. B. White and Jacques Barzun blamed television for the decline in students' abilities in the 1970s. "Short of throwing away all the television sets, I really don't know what we can do about writing," said White (qtd. in Sheils 60). Barzun was even more morose: "Letting the television just sink into [our] environment," "we have ceased to think with words" (qtd. in Sheils 60, 58).

At the same time that these comments were alerting the general public to a new literacy crisis, A. Bartlett Giamatti, president of Yale University, published an article in the *Yale Alumni Magazine* that received wide comment in academic circles. "[M]any Yale students cannot handle English—cannot make a sentence or a paragraph, cannot organize a paper, cannot follow through—well enough to do college work," bemoaned Giamatti in language remarkably like that of Harvard's Eliot a century before. This deterioration of language skills could be blamed on "people for whom Zen, the occult, Indians, organic gardening, Transcendental Meditation, the 'I Ching'—the whole frozen dinner of the new primitivism—were superior to words" (qtd. in Daniels 206, 207–8). As with the literacy crisis of 1896, not all educators perceived the situation in the same light. When Shelby Grantham set out to investigate the literacy crisis at Dartmouth for its alumni magazine in 1977, she could not find one to investigate. David J. Bradley, a writing teacher, declared, "There has been no decline in literacy among Dartmouth students in the 11 years I've been here." The chair of the history department, who had taught at Harvard as well, concurred: "I don't think there's any new crisis in writing." When the chair of the English department, the dean of the engineering school, a spokesperson for the medical school, and the staff in the admissions office offered similar comments, Grantham was forced to confess, "I had not expected such an answer, and I certainly had not expected it so consistently" (20). Bradley and James Heffernan, director of Dartmouth's freshman composition course, explained. " 'It's an autumnal rite, this handwringing about why Johnny can't write,' said the one, and the other concurred: 'The "crisis" isn't a crisis at all. These things have been said repeatedly before. It is a cyclical disturbance' " (21). With characteristic sarcasm, Harvey Daniels interprets the inconsistencies in Dartmouth's and Yale's reports on students' writing abilities in this way:

> Either the Dartmouth admissions boys have been aggressively out-recruiting Yale's, gathering in nearly all of the few remaining American teenagers who can speak and write, or else some element in the bracing New Hampshire air has helped the Dartmouth faculty to retain the perspective which teachers in other, more frantic locales have long since lost. (221)

Sheils's and Giamatti's views of the literacy crisis were not without critics. In "The Strange Case of Our Vanishing Literacy," Richard Ohmann called the literacy crisis detailed by *Newsweek, Time, Saturday Review*, the *Yale Alumni Magazine*, and others "a fiction, if not a hoax" (*Politics of Letters* 231). Countering the "quite varied evidence" found in these publications with evidence that reading scores for high school seniors between 1960 and 1970 had improved slightly, that Preliminary Scholastic Aptitude Test scores had twice increased between 1960 and 1972, and that the percentage of good writers among seventeen-year-olds had also increased, Ohmann confirmed what researchers from the Educational Testing Service and Office of Education had concluded: "We are now convinced that anyone who says he *knows* that literacy is decreasing . . . is at best unscholarly and at worse dishonest" (qtd. in Ohmann, *Politics of Letters* 232). But such critiques as Ohmann's did little to quiet critics of American schools and their students. Six years after *Newsweek's* "clarion call to literacy," *U.S. News & World Report*, in "Why Johnny Can't Write—and What's Being Done," used the parlance of war to describe the "counterattack" American schools were waging against the literacy crisis. *U.S. News* extolled their "weapons"—writing programs—which, Daniels contends, "taken as a group, reflect not a coherent and sensible national effort to upgrade student writing, but a fragmented, confused, and occasionally regressive collection of mixed-up schemes and tricked-up panaceas" (217–18).

Nevertheless, the United States was set to embark on another crusade for literacy.

CULTURAL VERSUS CRITICAL LITERACY

The "chorus of voices lamenting the decline in standards and foreseeing the end of Western civilization" has not been silenced (Ohmann, *Politics of Letters* 234). If one were to construct a continuum of current responses to the literacy crisis, E. D. Hirsch Jr.'s "Cultural Literacy List" might represent one pole and Paulo Freire's problem-posing critical literacy curriculum the other. Hirsch proposes to solve the literacy crisis, recapture the United States's economic preeminence, and eliminate the underclass by reinstating cultural unity through a shared national vocabulary or "cultural literacy." His cultural literacy list is composed of names, historical events, geographical places, and scientific terms that constitute "cultural literacy," that "middle ground" which "lies *above* the everyday levels of knowledge that everyone possesses and *below* the expert level known only to specialists" (*Cultural* 19). Although Hirsch acknowledges the political and economic side of cultural literacy, he insistently argues that cultural literacy is classless. On the one hand, he asserts that "illiterate and semiliterate Americans are condemned not only to poverty, but also to the powerlessness of incomprehension." Because they do not comprehend political issues, they seldom vote and become distrustful of the system "of which they are supposed to be the masters." Thus, the "civic importance of cultural literacy lies in the fact that true enfranchisement depends upon knowledge, knowledge upon literacy, and literacy upon cultural literacy" (12).

On the other hand, Hirsch counters objections that cultural literacy promotes the culture of the dominant class with the claim that "one of the main uses of a national vocabulary [which he defines as cultural literacy] is to enable effective and harmonious exchange despite personal, cultural and class differences," and he offers the standardization of public discourse in fifteenth- and sixteenth-century England as an example of the "inherently classless character of cultural literacy" (*Cultural* 104). Just as the literacy campaigns from 1800 to 1870 employed the public schools to overcome the threat that religious and ethnic diversity posed to cultural unity by inculcating common elements of American culture, so too does Hirsch look to the schools to effect "harmonious exchanges" among cultures by the inculcation of cultural literacy. Although he acknowledges the roles of family and church, Hirsch argues that "school is the traditional place for acculturating our children into our national life" because "it is the only institution that is susceptible to public policy control" (110). Hirsch was primarily concerned with second-ary education, but he hoped that his list of "What Every Literate American Should Know" would "create a sound edu-cation for later education in college" (275).

Freire's *Pedagogy of the Oppressed* represents the opposite end of responses to the literacy crisis. He contrasts his problem-posing education, with its "constant unveiling of reality," with what he calls a "banking concept of education," based on a "mechanistic, static, spatialized view of conscious-ness" (*Pedagogy* 68, 64). The difference between Freire's liberatory learning pedagogy and Hirsch's cultural literacy scheme is evidenced in Freire's rejection of pedagogies that ignore not only the social phenomenon of illiteracy but social phenomena in general. Unlike Hirsch, Freire argues that "merely teaching men to read and write does not work miracles; if there are not enough jobs for men able to work, teaching more men to read and write will not create them" ("Adult" 401). Moreover, in opposition to Hirsch's concept of a national vocabulary, Freire argues that "acquiring literacy does not involve memorizing sentences, words, or syllables— lifeless objects unconnected to an existential universe— but rather an attitude of creation and re-creation, a self-transformation producing a stance of intervention in one's context" (404).

Two different but interconnected approaches to Freire's theories can be heard in scholarship in the field of composi-tion studies. One approach has students examine their own experiences in order to understand how their language use has been shaped by previously unexamined assumptions about class, gender, culture, and especially previous schooling. Once students become aware of these dynamics, they can, in theory at least, become critically literate and see the possibility of change. Thomas J. Fox's study, which I analyze at some length in Chapter 2, is an example of this approach. The other approach attempts to demystify the conventions of academic discourse, ultimately moving students to critical consciousness of the ways groups make knowledge for their own purposes (Herzberg 115).

Patricia Bizzell and David Bartholomae have advanced this second approach. Their concerns are with basic writers, those "strangers in academia, unacquainted with the rules and rituals of college life, unprepared for the sorts of tasks their teachers were about to assign them" (Shaughnessy 3). Bizzell claims that their "salient characteristic" is their " 'outlandishness'—their appearance to many teachers and to themselves as the students who are most alien in the college community" ("What" 294). What makes these students strangers, Bizzell and Bartholomae argue, is their unfamiliarity with the conversations of academic discourse; in a sense, they need to be acculturated into "academic" literacy. As Bizzell explains, these students

> might be better understood in terms of their unfamiliarity
> with the academic discourse community, combined, perhaps,
> with such limited experience outside their native discourse
> communities that they are unaware that there is such a thing
> as a discourse community with conventions to be mastered.
> ("Cognition" 230)

To make academic discourse and its conventions more familiar to its strangers, Bartholomae suggests a "course of instruction . . . on a sequence of illustrated assignments [that] would allow for successive approximations of academic or 'disciplinary' discourse" (278). Similarly, Rose sees a university education as "an initiation into a variety of powerful ongoing discussions," and argues that underprepared students' initiation into it occurs "only through the repeated use of a new language in the company of others" (*Lives* 192). But as the literacy crusade enters the last decade of the twentieth century, some compositionists have begun to question this almost Platonic idea of academic discourse (Elbow, "Reflections"), and others have begun to chronicle the "violence" (Stuckey, Gilyard) that may ensue as students attempt to join an academic discourse community (Stuckey). Chapters 2, 3, and 4 of this study explore class, gender, and cultural dimensions of these concerns.

Bizzell and Bartholomae are among the most influential voices in the field of composition studies, but for all their influence, it is Hirsch's scheme for cultural literacy that has earned the attention of the media and the approbation of high-ranking officials in influential, public education circles. Furthermore, for all the English profession's denigration of Hirsch's cultural literacy scheme, it would be difficult to overestimate the influence of Hirsch's concept of cultural literacy on the profession of English itself. Bizzell, for example, notes the "unprecedented decision" of the Modern Language Association to devote its 1988 yearbook, *Profession 88*, "not to reprints but to articles invited to address a single theme: the cultural literacy work of Allan Bloom and E. D. Hirsch" ("Beyond" 665). In addition, Chester Finn (who now heads the National Assessment of Educational Programs) challenged the sixty conferees at the English Coalition Conference: Democracy Through Language (1987) to "catch up with the general public" and come up with a list of fifty to one hundred "core works of literature" that American schools should teach, assuring them that cultural literacy is an educational reform movement that English teachers can trust (Elbow, *What* 16).

One rather predictable effect of such a charge was the conferees' response, reported by Wayne Booth:

> Whether we were thinking of graduate students or of first graders, whether we had light teaching loads or heavy, whether we taught honors sections or remedial sections, whether our training was in linguistics, language arts, media studies, or critical theory, we knew that the last thing American educa-

Literacy Crises and Campaigns in Perspective   19

tion needs is one more collection of inert information, a nos-
trum to be poured raw into minds not actively engaged in
reading, thinking, writing, and talking. Not only did we believe
that abstracted lists of terms would not motivate our students
to become spontaneous learners; we were sure that they would
increase the tendency of too many of our schools to kill whatever spontaneity the children bring when they enter school.
(viii–ix)

Another predictable response to cultural literacy was the
tenor of the articles published in *Profession 88*: seven of the
eight articles condemned Hirsch's (and Bloom's) work on
cultural literacy for reasons similar to Booth's.

But this almost universal disaffection of teachers of
English for Hirsch and his scheme for cultural literacy belies
his influence on the profession of English. Let me explain my
contention. Both Bizzell and Booth agree that Hirsch is right
when he argues for background knowledge, for "in order
for people to share language, they must share knowledge"
(Bizzell, "Beyond" 662); Hirsch's "foundational" definition of
background knowledge and his scheme for inculcating it into
schoolchildren is what bothers most teachers of English. But
Bizzell is concerned that such "anti-foundationalist" critics
as William Buckley and James Sledd and Andrew Sledd offer
"no positive or utopian" alternative to Hirsch's scheme in
their responses in *Profession 88*. She fears that in the absence
of such alternatives, they "end up tacitly supporting the
political and cultural status quo" (667). In other words, by
refusing to provide alternate "lists" of their own, if you will,
critics of Hirsch's scheme unwittingly contribute to continuing calls from government officials and the "general public"
alike for its implementation.

In describing his experience at the English Coalition
Conference following Finn's and Hirsch's addresses, Peter
Elbow makes much the same point. Trying to provide, in
Bizzell's terms, a "utopian" alternative to Finn's demand,
Elbow and Robert Scholes proposed a short list of no more
than ten works that high school students should have read by
the time they graduate from high school. With just ten works,
they reasoned, a specific work's inclusion in or exclusion

from the list would not be "such a big deal." But, as Elbow reports, "no one would even nibble at our idea." "Such, perhaps, was the power of Hirsch's list and Finn's invitation. They put a hex—or we let them put a hex—on any possibility of leadership" (*What* 239–40). The refusal of the respondents in *Profession 88* to provide alternatives to Hirsch's scheme on the grounds that they have no "authority" seems another instance of this hex. In the absence of leadership, calls for implementation of Hirsch's scheme continue, especially for underprepared students. In a recent article in the *Journal of Basic Writing*, Donald Lazere, for one, argues for the implementation of Hirsch's cultural literacy because "many black and white students" have not stored up necessary background knowledge and thus find themselves "out of their element in the codes of academic discourse" ("Orality" 93).

LITERACY CRISES: LESSONS TO BE LEARNED

What lessons can be drawn from this short and admittedly selective comparison of literacy crises and campaigns in the United States in the nineteenth and twentieth centuries? For one, the perception that literacy is in a crisis of never before experienced dimensions is simply inaccurate. To believe otherwise is to fall prey to what Rose calls the "myth of transience," the belief that "if we can just do x or y, the problem [of illiteracy] will be solved—in five years, ten years, or a generation—and higher education will be able to return to its real work" ("Language" 355). Worse, such a belief obscures the failure of those remedies that were applied in the past and encourages application of similar remedies to the present. Just as the features of writing that dismayed Harvard president Eliot in 1871—"bad spelling," "ignorance of the simplest rules of punctuation"—were surface features to be remedied by college-level composition courses introduced in 1872, so, too, today's remedies for *no shared background* place a similar importance on the surface of things, in this case on the surface bits of knowledge and information which constitute a national vocabulary. Although Hirsch insists that "common background knowledge required for literacy does not depend on specific texts" ("Cultural Literacy" 1), both in his response to John Warnock (wherein he states, "to be culturally literate ... one does need to know a few facts about [specific texts]" [1]), and in his address to the English Coalition Conference (wherein he declares that reading Shakespeare's plays was not so important—reading "Lamb's Tales" would do as well [Elbow, *What* 17]), the belief that surface knowledge is all that is required to become culturally literate becomes all too clear. Finn's address to the Conference is another case in point, for he wanted a list of "core works of literature" that American schools should teach.

Furthermore, a comparison of the two crises not only makes clear the social, political, and economic issues underlying literacy campaigns but also makes clear that past campaigns failed because literacy was perceived as an invariant set of skills to be learned. As Russell and Berlin have pointed out, the literacy crusade of the last half of the nineteenth century did not succeed precisely because it singled out the use of a single dialect, that of the upper middle class, as the hallmark of literacy, thereby ignoring the needs of an increasingly diverse population.

As the twentieth century draws to a close and media reports of a literacy crisis continue, David Bleich, Carole Edelsky, and Ohmann are three of many scholars who insist that the current literacy campaign is likewise limited by a definition of literacy as an "invariant skill to be learned." Bleich argues for a social approach to literacy:

> [T]he study of literacy is an inquiry into how to say what matters to other people that matter.... Teachers and students have always been spontaneously important to one another, but the deep monastic, monadic, and individualist urge to depersonalize and decontextualize language use gradually paralyzes people's natural tendency to let human relationships shape language and knowledge.... [T]o socialize the classroom is to teach that each member has already brought a living literacy to class.... The classroom becomes a public place where each member sees that what each says both emerges from a history and participates in one, where literacy is created

by the exchange of language and the common pursuit of social purpose. (*Double* 330)

Ohmann and Edelsky likewise insist upon the social nature of literacy, but unlike those literacy crusaders of the nineteenth century who sought to establish a consensus-based social order founded on school-based literacy, they recognize that conflict as well as cooperation is an effect (and quite often a "teeth-gritting" effect) of literacy activities. Ohmann contends that literacy,

> like every other human activity or product . . . embeds social relations within it. And these relations always include *conflict* as well as cooperation. Like language itself, literacy is an exchange between classes, races, the sexes, and so on. (*Politics of English* 226)

Furthermore, Edelsky cautions that inviting the previously silenced voices of the poor, of Asians, of women into an exchange of language is oftentimes more complicated than those who seek to change and expand the standards of literacy realize:

> Each voice within these voices, however, is also a plurality— and not necessarily a harmonious plurality at that. There is great intra-individual conflict among the voices people internalize from a stratified society. . . . Attempting to merely add voices . . . ignores the contradictory, partial, "teeth-gritting" nature of each voice. (5)

It is to these conflicting exchanges between classes, genders, and cultures that this study of literacy now turns.

2

Re-Visioning Basic Writers

I remember sitting alone in the worn urban
classroom where my students [enrolled in the
SEEK Program at City College of New York]
had just written their first essays and where I
now began to read them, hoping to be able to
assess quickly the sort of task that lay ahead
of us that semester. But the writing was so
stunningly unskilled that I could not begin
to define the task nor even sort out the
difficulties. I could only sit there, reading and
re-reading the alien papers, wondering what had
gone wrong and trying to understand what I at
this eleventh hour of my students' academic
lives could do about it.
—Mina Shaughnessy, *Errors and Expectations*

Because basic writers are at the farthest remove from the
traditional college community, basic writing is an important
site of the literacy/illiteracy debate in postsecondary institutions in the United States. These are the "truly illiterate
among us," said one UCLA dean of students in UCLA's
English A—"bonehead English" in the parlance of professors
and students alike (Rose, *Lives* 2). Mina Shaughnessy's reaction to her first encounter with basic writing, quoted above,
is a classic among compositionists, and her response to it,
Errors and Expectations: A Guide for the Teacher of Basic

Writing, based upon her experiences at City College, "remains the most important single study of basic writers and their prose" (Moran and Jacobi 2).

In this chapter, I will explore basic writing as the site of the literacy/illiteracy debate, paying particular attention to the influence of Mina Shaughnessy on the seemingly contradictory voices she inspired: E. D. Hirsch Jr. on the one hand and Patricia Bizzell, David Bartholomae, and Mike Rose on the other. In particular, I will argue that although Bizzell, Bartholomae, and Rose have offered a much-needed corrective to Shaughnessy's essentialist view of language—a view that also informs Hirsch's scheme for cultural literacy—their own perceptions of basic writers as "disempowered lower class students" (Miller 172) is limited by their context, situated as they are in the academies of the privileged. Moreover, I will suggest that radical pedagogies designed to empower these basic writers may well be counterproductive in less competitive institutions.

THE LEGACY OF SHAUGHNESSY

In her ground-breaking *Errors and Expectations*, Shaughnessy successfully challenges the depiction of basic writers as "handicapped" or "disadvantaged," substituting instead the notion of basic writers as "beginners" who make mistakes "not because they are slow or non-verbal, indifferent to or incapable of academic excellence, but because they are beginners and must, like all beginners, learn by making mistakes" (5). Importantly, Shaughnessy identifies her beginners as "strangers in academia" who had "grown up in one of New York's ethnic or racial enclaves," "spoken other languages or dialects at home and never successfully reconciled the worlds of home and school" (3). Their unfamiliarity with the codes and conventions of academic discourse made it difficult for them to "cope with the books and lectures and papers that constitute the world of college." Thus, Shaughnessy argues, the basic writer has to acquire an "academic vocabulary," "a common language not only of the university but of the public and professional world outside" (187). This language becomes, in Shaughnessy's words, "a formidable yet solid fact to which the BW [basic writing] student must adjust—a 'given' " (224). Shaughnessy's concept of an "academic vocabulary" has provided much of the ground upon which opposing views of literacy, especially as they apply to basic writers, are situated.

Hirsch, himself, sees his scheme of cultural literacy as a logical extension of Shaughnessy's notion of an academic vocabulary (*Cultural Literacy* ix, 10). In language that echoes Shaughnessy's, Hirsch claims that "our national vocabulary" has, after a space of two hundred years, "common elements" of communication, elements decided by "history." No matter "how value-laden or partisan some of these common elements were in their origins long ago," he sees them as a given, as "the instruments through which we are able to communicate our views to one another and make decisions in a democratic way". Failing to teach students this national vocabulary has been a "fundamental educational mistake" and a "chief cause of illiteracy," Hirsch maintains (113).

Like Hirsch, several of the most influential compositionists currently writing about basic writers and academic literacy relate their pedagogies to Shaughnessy's concept of academic discourse. Bizzell, for one, places her theories firmly in the approach to academic discourse pioneered by Shaughnessy. Just as Shaughnessy points out that the problem basic writers have with persuasive discourse rests in their unfamiliarity with how much evidence they need to persuade an academic reader (270), so too does Bizzell contend that basic writers encounter difficulties with academic discourse because they are ignorant of the ways that "proof is defined in the various situations [they] must think and write in" ("Beyond" 662). In "Inventing the University," one of the most frequently mentioned articles in the field, Bartholomae cites Shaughnessy's notion of the advanced writer who is in a "constant tangle with the language" as the model for his contention that basic writers experience problems with academic discourse because they know the "key words" but not the sentence patterns of academic discourse (284). In an endnote, he acknowledges the influence of Bizzell as well, stating that his "debt to Bizzell's work should be evident everywhere in this essay" (433).

Shaughnessy's legacy is apparent in Rose's work, too. In "The Language of Exclusion," he points out that it was Shaughnessy who "got us to see that even the most error-ridden prose arises from the confrontation of inexperienced student writers with the complex linguistic and rhetorical expectations of the academy" (357). Moreover, he applauds Bartholomae's and Bizzell's approach to writing instruction:

> We need to define our work as transitional or initiatory, orient-ing or socializing to what David Bartholomae and Patricia Bizzell call the academic discourse community. This redefini-tion is not just romantic sleight-of-hand. If truly adopted, it would require us to reject a medical-deficit model of language, to acknowledge the rightful place of all freshmen in the acad-emy, and once and for all to replace loose talk about illiteracy with more precise and pedagogically fruitful analysis. We would move from a mechanistic focus on error toward a de-manding curriculum that encourages the full play of language activity and that opens out onto the academic community rather than sequestering students from it. (358)

What the foregoing discussion illustrates is that the embattled (and embittered) sides in the literacy/illiteracy debate do, in fact, share a common ground, a legacy from Shaughnessy, a belief that students need to be initiated into a discourse community. Moreover, as Rose points out, both proponents of cultural literacy (Hirsch, Chester Finn, William Bennett, and Mortimer Adler, among others) and Bizzell, Bartholomae, and Rose, himself, who oppose them, "boldly challenge" prevailing assumptions that underprepared students are incapable of negotiating anything other than a "mediocre and grinding curriculum" (*Lives* 233–34).

A CRITIQUE OF THE LEGACY OF SHAUGHNESSY

Shaughnessy's *Errors and Expectations*, based on her own experiences, has encouraged other instructors of basic writing to see their basic writing students' difficulties with academic discourse as evidence not of mental sluggishness but of unfamiliarity with the rules of academic discourse and the use of a home language not valued by the academy. Both of these explanations can be viewed as the effects of class, for the underprepared students Shaughnessy taught were from "ethnic or racial enclaves" whose residents had been previously excluded from the privileges of higher education. Researchers who followed Shaughnessy's lead took one of two approaches. Those who sought to investigate the cognitive processes that writers employ when faced with a writing task generally ignored the influence of class on students' composing processes, envisioning the student as a "presexual, preeconomic, prepolitical person" (Miller 87).[3] However, their attempts to characterize basic writers in a single developmental model failed because the "diversity and depth" of basic writers' backgrounds make them "too protean to be captured by any single psychological model" (Lunsford and Sullivan 22).

In the early 1980s, those followers of Shaughnessy who sought to familiarize basic writers with the codes and conventions of academic discourse began to question this cognitive approach to basic writing. In 1982 and 1983, for example, Marilyn Cooper and Michael Holzman, Robert J. Connors, John Clifford, and Bizzell, among others, published articles especially critical of the work of Linda Flower and fellow researcher John Hayes.[4] Bizzell was one of the first to criticize cognitive-based models for ignoring the contexts in which writing takes place, arguing that "all writing is context bound, and therefore cannot be adequately described by universal models" ("College" 205). Furthermore, she charges that such cognitive models as Flower and Hayes's "prejudge those unequally prepared for school as unequal in mental development" (196). Drawing upon the work of Freire, Bizzell concludes that basic writers need "critical training to trace their victimage to social forces rather than to 'fate,' and hence to work toward control of their own social destinies" (196). The way to empower students, maintains Bizzell, is to admit them "into the academic discourse community" and into "the abstracting, formalizing power of academic work [that] enables us to understand our experience in ways not made available by common sense or folk wisdom" (206).

In a series of essays, Bizzell applies a similar critique to Hirsch's appropriation of Shaughnessy's work with basic writers to legitimate his "dream for a national curriculum." In "Arguing about Literacy," she contends that Hirsch "systematically suppresses" and detaches his core curriculum "from its own social origins," "forgetting to mention that the turn-of-the-century lists he admires were first promulgated by Harvard, a highly race-, sex-, and class-determined institution." Furthermore, she argues, he conceals the inherent discrimination in his core curriculum by deferring to the "impersonal force of history" (146–47). Building upon the assumption that all writing is context bound, Bizzell points out that Shaughnessy's advice to "get student writing to approximate a set of well-known and accepted academic models" and Hirsch's advice to initiate all citizens into "a predetermined or 'given' national discourse community" both rest upon a "unitary conception of what academic discourse should be" and into which "all student—and professional— writing must fit" ("Beyond" 662–63). For Bizzell, the health of the discourse community lies in its very ability to adapt to context, to "changing historical conditions" (663).

Bartholomae is another influential critic of cognitive-based pedagogies. Flower's "Revising Writer-Based Prose," published in the *Journal of Basic Writing*, garners much of Bartholomae's criticism in his oft-quoted "Inventing the University." To Bartholomae, Flower's concept of basic writing as "writer-based prose," or "the interior monologue of a writer thinking and talking to himself," and her solution, teaching students to revise with readers in mind, seem almost hopelessly "pastoral" in their oversimplification of the relationship between writer and audience (276). What Flower denies, Bartholomae claims, is the situation in the classroom—"the central problem of academic writing"—namely, that the audience (the teacher) knows more about the subject and about writing than does the student (277). Revision is not the answer to basic writers' difficulties with academic discourse, Bartholomae says; rather, helping students to become "insiders," even if that means that they must, at first, "crudely mimic the 'distinctive register' of academic discourse," is (284).

Just as Rose and Bizzell have argued in the foregoing discussions, Bartholomae exhorts teachers to resist practices that locate basic writers outside the academy, thereby excluding them from full participation in it. His text, *Facts, Artifacts, and Counterfacts*, co-written with Anthony R. Petrosky, offers a particular example of what he means. Although their text is for basic writers, Bartholomae and Petrosky make clear that the text could serve for an honors class as well. That is as it should be, they contend, for "there was no good reason to take students who were not fluent readers and writers and consign them to trivial or mechanical work in the belief that it would somehow prepare them for a college education" (n.p.).

Like Bartholomae, Rose is concerned about cognitive studies that place basic writers (and readers) outside the academy by suggesting that they "think in fundamentally different ways from the insiders" ("Narrowing" 267). Such cognitive reductionism, he explains, although intended to be value free, is "anything but neutral." In fact, Rose claims, "social and political hierarchies end up encoded in sweeping cognitive dichotomies." Rose concludes that the field of composition needs "an increased sensitivity to the social forces that shape cognitive activity" (297). He reiterates this conclusion in " 'This Wooden Shack Place,' " a 1990 article coauthored with Glynda Hull, wherein they acknowledge their longstanding efforts to "integrate social-cultural and cognitive approaches to better understand the institutional and classroom practices that contribute to students being designated remedial" (287).

Another, self-proclaimed "urgent" critique of *Errors and Expectations*, occasioned in part by the "popular success" of Hirsch's cultural literacy proposals, points out that the essentialist view of language that underpins basic writing pedagogy underpins Shaughnessy's perception of academic discourse as necessary and advantageous (Lu, "Redefining" 34). This privileging of academic discourse is in urgent need of critique, contends Min-zhan Lu, especially "when viewed in the popular success of E. D. Hirsch Jr.'s proposals for 'educational reforms' " (37). She urges those compositionists interested in examining writing in "relation to the politics of gender, race, nationality and class" to forestall Hirsch's "self-conscious" use of Shaughnessy's work and to acknowledge Shaughnessy's essentialist view of language as the "most limiting aspect" of her pedagogy (38). Later in this chapter, I will show how Bartholomae's and Bizzell's work has been subject to the same critique.

All in all, Bizzell, Bartholomae, Rose, and Lu point out that the pedagogies advanced by Shaughnessy, Hirsch, and Flower and Hayes rely upon an oversimplified view of language and literacy acquisition, one that ignores the social contexts of both, and their concomitant failure to consider the social relationships embedded in all discussions of language and literacy. Moreover, the discussions of basic writing described above often focus on class as a marginalizing factor, precisely because most basic writing research has focused on Shaughnessy's "alien" students—minorities and those first-generation college students whose parents are lower-class workers. Importantly, instead of focusing on students actually enrolled in basic writing classes, basic writing research has attempted to define basic writers in terms of "common socio-economic backgrounds and shared educational experiences" (Lunsford and Sullivan 18). Finally, a common theme underlies the pedagogies of Bizzell and Bartholomae in particular. On the one hand, they seek to empower basic writers both by making them aware of social structures that privilege academic discourse and by initiating basic writers into the conventions and structures of academic discourse. On the other hand, they want to expand the notion of academic discourse to include the habits of language and rhetorical developments that marginalized writers bring with them to the writing classroom.

In the rest of this chapter, I will further Bizzell's, Bartholomae's, and Rose's critiques of acontextual studies of language and literacy to the conversations about basic writing that take place in the context of composition circles. I will argue that the dominant voices are situated in the academies of the privileged, that this situation skews their and the field's perceptions of basic writers, and that pedagogies derived from this reified notion of the basic writer are limited and limiting.

SAYING SOMETHING THAT MATTERS

"Their salient characteristic is their outlandishness—their appearance to many teachers and to themselves as the students who are most alien in the college community" (Bizzell, "What" 294). Bizzell's assessment of basic writers in "What Happens When Basic Writers Come to College?" is echoed repeatedly in conversations about basic writing today. I want to examine the "literacy discourse community" of the most influential journals of composition scholarship, paying particular attention to Bizzell's idea that we must "adopt a rhetorical perspective," to create literacy through "the inter-action of the professor's and the students' cultural resources" ("Arguing" 150). I am going to look closely at the professors' cultural resources—their situations in the academies of the privileged.

Bizzell, Rose, and Bartholomae are among the most frequently cited scholars writing about basic writers in the most respected journals in composition studies. (In review essays collected in *Research in Basic Writing*, Bartholomae is cited eighteen times, Rose fifteen times, and Bizzell nine times; only Shaughnessy and Lunsford are cited as often as Bartholomae.) The academies where they make their academic homes are, respectively, the University of Pittsburgh, UCLA, and the College of the Holy Cross. All three of these institutions are included in *Peterson's Competitive Colleges: 1991–92*. In its introductory "A Note to Students," *Peterson's* defines "the primary parameters" it uses to identify "competitive" colleges: "the percentages of freshmen scoring in *each centile* on the SAT verbal and math portions or in particular ranges on the ACT and the percentages coming from the top tenth of their high school class" (v). Of the more than 3,400 accredited degree-granting institutions of higher education in the United States, just 363 colleges and universities are listed. Furthermore, fewer than 50 of these 363 accept under 50 percent of their applicants (Finn 113); Holy Cross and UCLA are included in this elite group. Despite differences in size, mission, and cost, their salient characteristic is the presence on their campuses of a large percentage of high-achieving students (based on national tests and high school achievement) (*Peterson's* v).

The College of the Holy Cross, where Bizzell, a professor of English, directs the Writing Across the Curriculum Program, is a Jesuit college of some 2,700 students located in Worcester, Massachusetts. *The Holy Cross Catalog* claims that "it is one of the best liberal arts colleges in the United States," "educating the best and the brightest to be tomorrow's leaders" (3). A profile of those students accepted in 1990 supports this claim. Only 43 percent of those students who applied for admission in 1990 were accepted, and of those, 60 percent were from the top tenth of their high school graduating class. Thirty-one percent of the incoming freshman class received scores of 600 or above on the verbal portion of the SAT, while 60 percent achieved those scores in math. Tuition costs at Holy Cross are high: $15,530 for the 1991–1992 school year ("Facts" A33); minority students account for about 10 percent of the incoming student enrollment. Bizzell does not define the basic writers of whom she speaks in terms of SAT scores or high school rank. But her description in "Arguing about Literacy" may come close to her experiences of basic writers, especially as they might appear at Holy Cross (or at Rutgers, her earlier home of like student demographics): "These challenges of academic literacy typically come from social groups at some remove from the upper classes—that is, from the lower classes, foreign-born, non-white, and/or female" (141). Given the upper-middle to upper-class backgrounds of the students at Holy Cross and the small number of minorities enrolled, is it any wonder that basic writers appear at some remove from the upper classes and as "outlanders"?

Rose is Associate Director of Writing Programs at UCLA where, as at Holy Cross, fewer than half of those who apply are admitted. Again, SAT scores of incoming freshmen are similar to those of Holy Cross's students: 23 percent of the incoming freshman class had verbal SAT scores of 600 or above, and 63 percent had math scores of 600 or above. Size, tuition, and minority enrollments at UCLA are vastly different from those at Holy Cross, however. UCLA's total enrollment is more than fifteen times that of Holy Cross, and minorities (Asian Americans, Native Americans, Hispanics, and African Americans), taken as a whole, comprise a majority. In-state tuition for the 1991–1992 school year was $1,180 ("Facts" A31). The basic writers Rose describes in " 'This Wooden Shack Place' " seem to be at some remove from those he writes about in *Lives on the Boundary*. The basic writers in " 'This Wooden Shack Place,' " identified as "at-risk" students based upon test scores, are in the "most remedial composition class at UCLA." This particular class had students whose SAT verbal scores ranged from 220 to 400 (288). At UCLA, these particular students must seem like "strangers in a strange land," the phrase Rose used to describe the veterans he taught (*Lives* 142). Given the situation of these students in the overall context of UCLA, it is small wonder that the UCLA dean quoted at the beginning of this chapter found them the "truly illiterate among us." But the students at UCLA whose stories Rose chronicles in *Lives on the Boundary* more often than not have high school records of success and "little experience of being on the academic fringe" (173). Perhaps readers of this award-winning book overlook this distinction, thereby conflating Rose's history as "voc ed" student with the histories of those students his book reports. At any rate, not all basic writing students at UCLA are alike, but the most memorable ones appear as strangers in a strange land, much as Rose appeared when he first enrolled at UCLA as a graduate student.

Bartholomae's University of Pittsburgh is not so easily described. Although included in *Peterson's*, no data are available, for instance, on either the percentage of applicants accepted for the 1990–1991 academic year or on the percentage of entrants whose scores were 600 or above on the SAT verbal and math tests. However, the University's most recent catalog describes admissions as "competitive"; additionally, the committee on admissions "carefully studies each applicant's secondary school record, performance on college entrance examinations," and a nebulous category called "personal qualifications" (1). Moreover, *Peterson's* does show that 27 percent of the 1990–1991 freshman class were in the top 10 percent of their high school graduating classes. Pittsburgh's minority enrollment is about the same as Holy Cross's (10 percent), but its in-state tuition of $4,660 ("Facts" A35), while high for a state university, is considerably less than that of Holy Cross. At the beginning of *Facts, Artifacts, and Counterfacts*, Bartholomae (then professor of English and Director of Composition) and Petrosky describe the students for whom they originally designed this course in 1977 as "minority or special-admission students," "students outside the mainstream" (4). Interestingly, in a footnote, they mention that currently "there is a larger percentage of white, regular-admission students taking the course than there was when we began" (41).

The point I want to make with all these facts and figures is that the pervasiveness of the perception of basic writers as outsiders comes from the fact that they *are* outsiders in the context of the academies in which basic writing's most influential spokespersons are situated. Secondly, our ideas about basic writing and particularly our ideas of the influence of class on basic writing are skewed by the fact that many of the students enrolled in basic writing courses at Holy Cross, UCLA, and the University of Pittsburgh are "disempowered lower-class students," frequently admitted as "special students." What we neglect to note is that many of Rose's underprepared and Bartholomae's "outsiders" might very well be placed in regular composition classes in less competitive colleges and open-admissions community colleges. Simply stated, the portrait of basic writing students painted in broad strokes in many journal articles is a portrait of a very specific group of basic writing students housed within the halls of America's most competitive colleges and universities. Yet the metaphor of "basic writers" as outsiders persists. Susan Wall and Nicholas Coles, who were participants in the development of the course described in *Facts, Artifacts, and Counterfacts*, comment upon the pervasiveness of the metaphor and speculate as to its source. Noting, as I have done as well, the acknowledged indebtedness of Rose, Bartholomae, and Bizzell to Shaughnessy, Wall and Coles speculate that the metaphor came into the discourse by way of *Errors and Expectations*. I concur. Furthermore, they mention that Shaughnessy's metaphor of "true outsiders" comes from her first experience with basic writing. Her reaction provides the epigraph of this chapter. Wall and Coles's caution is important to note as well. As they maintain, Shaughnessy's "more seasoned and characteristic view" of basic writers and their struggles is the "dictum" that "the struggles of basic writers are the struggles of all writers 'writ large' " (244).

Cherryl Armstrong makes a similar point in "Re-examining Basic Writing: Lessons from Harvard's Basic Writers," wherein she contends that "basic writers' problems are problems basic to writing" (70). Lest one think that Armstrong is talking of special admissions students, let me permit her to describe the students in what would seem an improbable course, *basic* writing (my emphasis) at Harvard: the students were "often advanced placement English students at their high schools or prep schools" who "had no trouble writing because they were unprepared for the university"—"many of them had been preparing for schools such as Harvard all their lives" (70, 76). In fact, Armstrong's basic writers were ranked among "the most outstanding freshmen in the country" (76). Her contention that "basic" is a relative term (one that ought to be done away with altogether [69]) reiterates the one that Lynn Troyka, former editor of the *Journal of Basic Writing*, makes in "Defining Basic Writers in Context," an essay collected in Theresa Enos's *A Sourcebook for Basic Writing Teachers*, "the single most important collection of essays in the field" (Moran and Jacobi 7). In this essay, Troyka, like Wall and Coles and Armstrong, cautions that the basic writing field is building generalizations about basic writers upon experiences with isolated individual programs. Reporting on her national study of what typifies basic writing, Troyka concludes that the term "basic writing" as portrayed in professional journals does not cover the enormous diversity among basic writers. Furthermore, her research suggests that basic writers differ from college to college and may even differ from year to year within a single college or university (13). (Bartholomae and Petrosky likewise mentioned the change in the kinds of students assigned to their basic writing course from the time they designed it to the time they published *Facts, Artifacts, and Counterfacts*.) As Lunsford and Sullivan conclude in their review essay,

> This national study holds important implications for future efforts to define basic writers in context because it shifts the thrust of our research from attempts to analyze the students' "common" cultural heritage to an explanation of their social and linguistic diversity. (20)

I am arguing that social relationships embedded in conversations in the field's professional journals contribute to this skewed portrait of the basic writer and make it difficult to define basic writers in context. Let me explain. Bizzell's, Bartholomae's, and Rose's voices are heard in *College English* and *College Composition and Communication*, with readerships, in 1988, of 16,000 and 11,000 respectively (Anson and Miller 202). Armstrong's article and Troyka's essay, both of which point to the reified and inaccurate portrait of basic writers, are published in the *Journal of Basic Writing* (readership 2,000+ [Anson and Miller 206]) and Enos's collection respectively. Although Enos's *Sourcebook* is arguably the "single most important collection of essays on basic writing," I wonder about the extent of Troyka's influence. My own experience makes me suspect that it is rather limited. At the University of Nevada, Las Vegas, where I direct the freshman (*sic*) composition program, I schedule twenty-five sections of English A each semester, yet the university's library has no copy of Enos's work. Thus the dominant picture of the basic writer in the most influential journals remains that of the outsider, precisely because those writers, more often than not, are outsiders in the academies that provide the contexts for their instruction. Moreover, social relationships embedded in the institutional structures of higher education make it unlikely that other voices will soon be able to say "what matters to other people that matter" (Bleich, *Double* 330).

According to *Profession 91*, 344,000 students were enrolled in "remedial and developmental" composition in two-year colleges in 1988; 184,000 students were enrolled in these same courses in four-year institutions ("Franklin" 4). What is puzzling to that journal's editor is the 7.5 percent decline in enrollment in these courses in four-year institutions vis-à-vis a 21.6 percent increase in enrollment in these classes in two-year institutions in the period from 1985 to 1988 (1). It is important to note that almost twice as many basic writing students are enrolled in courses in two-year colleges, and if the apparent trend of declining enrollment in four-year colleges continues, the gap between enrollment in two-year colleges and four-year institutions will widen, reinforcing the position of the two-year college as the primary site of basic writing instruction, and the site of very little conversation about basic writing in professional journals.

"Is There a Writing Program in This College? Two Hundred and Thirty-six Two-Year Schools Respond," a recent article published in *College Composition and Communication*, addresses this issue. Although two-year colleges teach approximately one-half of all students taking any kind of composition course, no major study of their writing programs has been published since the National Council of Teachers of English and College Composition and Communication Report, *English in the Two-Year College*, was released in 1965 (five years before Shaughnessy's aliens appeared on college campuses). As a result, pictures of the two-year college are frequently formed on experiences of just one or two institutions. But this study shows not only that no model of writing program emerges, but more importantly, the two-year colleges form "interpretive communities developed with different missions, purposes and objectives from the communities of those who teach in colleges and universities where majors, programs, and graduate degrees abound" (Raines 152, 154).

Clearly, it is important to hear from practitioners in the two-year colleges. Keith Kroll, however, shows how seldom

English faculty in two-year colleges contribute even to their own journal, *Teaching English in the Two-Year College*. He reports that in 1988, not only did community college faculty write only 38 percent of the articles published in that journal, they also contributed only 33 percent of the submissions. Their voices were even less apparent in *College English* and *College Composition and Communication*. Volumes 38, 39, and 40 of *College Composition and Communication* had just one article and six "Staffroom Interchanges" written by two-year college teachers. For the 1986 year, only 3 percent of the articles submitted to *College English* were from two-year college faculty (105). As a consequence of this silence, teachers in research universities dominate the conversation in professional journals. Both Helon Howell Raines and Mary Kupiec Cayton argue that much of this silence can be attributed to the part-time, marginalized status of two-year-college teachers. In terms borrowed from Bartholomae, Cayton dubs part-timers the "outsiders" in academic discourse. As she explains, "For a part-time or temporary faculty member, who remains an outsider to the working of the profession in very basic ways, comfort with the academic vernacular can remain tantalizingly out of reach" ("Writing" 650). Raines agrees, claiming that the voices of teachers in two-year colleges, whether the teachers are part time or full time, "are sometimes silenced because we do not compose in the academic discourse of our colleagues in the universities" (159).

As the foregoing discussion illustrates, class does affect academic discourse. In competitive colleges and universities, where students are placed in basic writing classes on the weakness of their performances on standardized tests, the correlation between low test scores and socio-economic status (see Stuckey, 116–24, for an angry account of this correlation) suggests that the problems these students encounter when they negotiate the conventions of academic discourse can be attributed to the lower-class literacies they bring with them to upper middle-class institutions. Moreover, because teachers of most basic writing courses are as marginalized within their own academic discourse community as the students whom they teach are in theirs, a reified, inaccurate portrait of the basic writer as "outsider," as "disempowered lower-class student," continues to be painted, relatively unchallenged, in the most influential journals in the field. Such a perception blinds us to the fact that basic writers' problems are shared by many of the students sitting in regular writing classrooms in less competitive institutions. Furthermore, this picture painted in too bold strokes leads to pedagogies of empowerment which are limited and limiting as a result of this unitary conception of the basic writer as lower-class student.

EMPOWERING STUDENTS

"Empowerment" is a buzzword in scholarly conversations among compositionists, but the first discussions of empowerment were directed toward empowering basic writers. Not surprisingly, Freire's work with illiterates in Brazil was imported by Marxist scholars, in particular, as a way of empowering basic writing "illiterates," whom Bizzell designates as "politically oppressed" ("College" 196) and as "outlanders" ("What" 294).

Two different but interconnected conversations about empowering basic writers can be heard in journals and conferences. One, as represented by Bizzell, Bartholomae, and Rose, in particular, argues that basic writers are "sequestered" from the academy (Rose, "Language" 358) and need to "learn to speak our language, to speak as we do, to try on the peculiar ways of knowing, selecting, evaluating, reporting, concluding, and arguing that define the . . . *various* discourses in our community" (Bartholomae 336). Because academic discourse is the discourse of power, students will be empowered when they master it. The other conversation, represented by David Bleich and Tom Fox among others, argues that such a pedagogy uncritically privileges academic discourse and maintains that writing be examined in relation to the politics of class, gender, and race. Once students become aware of these dynamics, they can become critically literate and can see the possibility of change.

As I have suggested, one of the critical differences

between Hirsch's appropriation of Shaughnessy on the one hand and Bizzell's, Bartholomae's, and Rose's on the other is Hirsch's acceptance of her essentialist view of language and Bizzell's, Bartholomae's, and Rose's extension of it. But Bizzell, Bartholomae, and Rose, like Shaughnessy, have been criticized for privileging academic discourse. Bizzell, to be fair, does take into account the risks students take when joining a new discourse community, but she feels that "because of the hegemonic power of the academic world view, [students] will also find its acquisition well worth the risks" ("What" 301). More importantly, Bizzell has modified her position. In her most recent work, Bizzell says that she is now "trying to modify" her position that justifies teaching academic discourse on the grounds that acquisition of its codes enables students to "be better equipped to improve their lot in life" ("Professing" 317). In addition, she admits that while she once may have perceived Hirsch's position as "the antithesis of my own," she now recognizes him as her "dark double" and confesses that, at times, "I came close to doing just what I condemn Hirsch for doing in his specification of a national cultural literacy: I set myself up as an expert who could in fact undertake such a task unilaterally" (*Academic* 29).

Perhaps Bizzell's reading of J. Elspeth Stuckey's *The Violence of Literacy* has led her to the realization that the world of Holy Cross is not the world at large, that her pronouncements about the benefits and power of academic discourse have been influenced by her position as one of the "comfortably ensconced" among others just as comfortable ("Professing" 321). But for the basic writers at institutions like Holy Cross, Bizzell's pronouncements about the benefits of literacy probably ring true. As Victor Villanueva Jr. argues, minority students are "in school to fulfill a dream, a longtime American dream of success through education. They [are] not in school to have their dreams destroyed" (256). Moreover, as Donald Lazere points out, elected lower-class students admitted to elite universities are "more receptive" to the "leftist critical pedagogy" that Bizzell promotes "for many reasons including the facts that elite colleges select from among the brightest of them and have more resources than nonelite schools for recruiting, financial aid, tutoring, and counseling" ("Back" 18).

Additional critiques of Bizzell's scholarship appear in articles questioning Bartholomae's pedagogy. Richard Boyd cautions that the idea of mimeticism inherent in Bartholomae's pedagogy sets up a kind of "master/slave" relationship where the "student-as-mimic" is "relegated to a perpetually subordinate role." That student/teacher relationship is a far cry from the one envisioned in Freire's " 'pedagogy of knowing,' where teacher and student are joined together as equals in [as Ira Shor describes] a 'loving, humble, trusting, critical' educational endeavor aimed at liberating all parties from the structures that oppress them, including the dominant discourses" (342). Cayton points out, too, that in mimicking the discourse of the academy, students are asked to mimic stylistically the values of the bureaucracy at the same time academic discourse tries to critique those very values ("Writing" 652). Wall and Coles question this same stance in Bartholomae's pedagogy, maintaining that Bartholomae attempts to initiate students into academic discourse while trying to encourage them to critique it from their marginalized position in the academy. Ultimately, they conclude that "this interaction, this attainment of a consciously marginal and critical stance, remains more a promise of his pedagogy than anything he demonstrates in his work to date" (234). On a quite different note, Sheryl I. Fontaine, John Peavoy, and Susan Hunter assert that Bartholomae's pedagogy (and Bizzell's as well) is potentially weakened for "a significant portion of the college population," those regularly admitted students at academically competitive undergraduate colleges "where the language of the academy may not be coveted for its power and prestige" (2).

Much of the critique of this strand of conversation, which seeks to empower basic writers by initiating them into the conventions of academic discourse, comes from the other strand, which seeks instead to demystify academic discourse by uncovering the psychological and political motivations underlying its "superiority." Rather than helping students to "develop the writing strategies that are an intimate part of academic inquiry and what has come to be called critical literacy—comparing, synthesizing, analyzing" (Rose, *Lives* 193–94), this academic inquiry and the discourse used to express its findings bear "the usual social and epistemological marks of the masculine academy," Bleich points out in *The Double Perspective* (55). By the time students arrive in postsecondary institutions, Bleich explains, social relations in the classroom have become so desocialized that language is seen as contacts between individuals rather than as "between communities with continuously varying mutual interests" (6). Drawing upon Richard Ohmann, Bleich argues that the academy's goal of suppressing language's social character is related to the "cultural-economic" demand for a "static social class structure" (12). Thus, academic writing becomes a standardized writing which, along with its concomitant view of a standardized literacy, Bleich maintains, has roots in a centuries-old, Western, exclusive, totally male academy (78). He proposes a socialized classroom in its stead.

Chapters 7 through 10 of *The Double Perspective* comprise a case study of Bleich's attempt to socialize the classroom in a generic literature and composition course that he taught and named "Studying One's Own Language." Because Bleich believes that a social concept of literacy cannot be envisioned *"without also making the corresponding change in the social relations of the classroom"* (172), he restructured this classroom so that authority rested with student subgroups and discussion groups as well as with the instructor. While traditional first-year courses require students to write argumentative discourse, to persuade or inform some imaginary audience, the emphasis in Bleich's course was

> first on expressing, articulating, and sharing, and then on using one's own and others' insight to develop a more sophisticated analytical understanding of one's own and others' use of language. I have tried to translate some of the aims of ordinary but serious conversation among people who care about one another into a disciplined mode of collectively inquiring into language use and literacy. (191)

I have described Bleich's course in some detail for three reasons. First, Bleich's focus on gender relations is an important backdrop to Chapter 3 of this study. Elizabeth A. Flynn, for example, regards Bleich's work in *The Double Perspective* as an excellent example of the "recuperative work that identifies tendencies within the field" of composition studies that are "compatible with feminism" ("Composition" 150). Second, the book has been well-received among compositionists. Joyce Irene Middleton, in her review in *College Composition and Communication*, calls *The Double Perspective* "an important book that stimulates interest and encourages inquiry in language theory and in the interrelatedness of writing (speaking), reading (listening), thinking, and rhetoric" (233). (This interrelatedness is the focus of the final chapter of this study as well.) Third, Bleich's course provides the theoretical rationale for Fox's *The Social Uses of Writing*, a work I will critique in some detail in the remaining pages of this chapter. (Fox explains his indebtedness to Bleich, Bartholomae, Bizzell, and Kenneth Bruffee in the first few pages of his book.) I want to extend Middleton's critique of Bleich's method to Fox's method as well, suggesting that isolating class, gender, and race provides a limited view of social relations in the classroom and that his isolation of class, in particular, leads students to see themselves as "unique individuals" rather than as members of a community trying to say something that matters to others that matter.

As Middleton argues, Bleich's argument is limited by his use of response statements from male and female students to show the force of gender relations on language use. She problematizes his "generic inferences about male readers," wondering how minority males would react to Bleich's conclusions that the generic male reader is psychologically distant from reading and needs complete literal comprehension (232). This same limitation is even more apparent in Fox's study, wherein he isolates class and race, as well as gender, in studying students' language uses, ignoring the interaction of these three factors. Furthermore, Gordon P. Thomas finds the pedagogy Fox proposes—one intended to "lead students to become more tolerant of and sympathetic toward disadvantaged groups" (220)—"troubling" because it is "disproportionately ambitious" on the one hand and because it glosses over "the teaching of what seems to me an important aspect of introductory composition: the teaching of academic prose" on the other (222).

Fox describes the concern of his book as a whole as

> the exploration of how students' memberships in social groups influence their language use in the classroom and an argument for a pedagogy that will work against [the] sense of exclusion that many working class, black, and women students feel in education. (90)

The assignments, described in the appendix, ask students to examine the influence of gender, class, and race on their language use by responding to such readings as Susan Glaspell's "A Jury of Her Peers," Zora Neale Hurston's *Their Eyes Were Watching God*, and Rebecca Harding Davis's *Life in the Iron Mills*. Additionally, students are required to write four analytical essays: comparing their language systems first with one then with the other member of their subgroup; summarizing the effects of social and economic class on their language systems; and, in a final essay, describing and explaining the roles gender, race, and social class play in their language use (123–26).

Chapters 3, 4, and 5 present four case studies, two demonstrating the effects of gender on students' language use, one demonstrating the effects of working class background on a male student's language use, and the last describing the effects of race on a female black student's language use. I am going to examine, in particular, Fox's study of "Mr. H," included in Chapter 3, "Gender Interests in Reading and Writing." Fox's separate considerations of gender, class, and race have led him, I believe, to walk right up to a class-influenced response in Mr. H's work and miss it. But more important than what I perceive to be Fox's misreading is the inherent problem in any discussion of class in American classrooms, a problem that this case study illuminates. In Stuckey's words, "the idea of a class structure is uncomfortable for many Americans" (1). Class structure is an especially uncomfortable idea for first-year college students. I am suggesting that when they are confronted with its existence, they will deny its existence, retreating into "unique individual" postures, thereby reinforcing a sense of exclusion, but this time, exclusion from the interactive literacy community that Fox is trying to promote.

Fox is careful to note that he did not intend his case studies to portray "representative" students (49), but, as Thomas aptly points out, the case studies seem meant to illustrate how Fox's pedagogy, by making students more aware of their language use patterns, will enable students to change them (221). In truth, Fox's pedagogy may reinforce the very behavior that he is trying to change.

The Case of "Mr. H"

I want to take a closer look at Mr. H's case study. The head to the study reads "Competition, Persuasion, and Masculinity." Fox investigates Mr. H's description of males as "tough and independent," interpreting these traits as stereotypically masculine, but also as consciously chosen. As Fox explains, Mr. H characteristically "presents himself as autonomous, self-controlled, master of his self and his surroundings" (61). For all his mastery of self and situation, however, whenever Mr. H is confronted with a hierarchy in which he is at a disadvantage, he reveals another contradictory sense of self, one that is "embarrassed, degraded, and occasionally out of control" (64). Fox concludes that "the sense of competition, . . . the anger at subjection, the sense of confidence in language use ('I write the way I feel' . . .) all are products of the ideology of masculinity" (70). I am contending that they are just as likely products of the ideology of social class.

It is unfortunate that in relegating Mr. H's case to the chapter devoted to the influences of gender, Fox has included neither Mr. H's response to Essay 8, which asks students to "recall an experience where you realized that you were from a different social or economic class than someone else," nor Mr. H's response to Analytical Paper 3, wherein students are asked to "summarize your understanding of how social and economic class influence your language system" (125). I am wondering if those responses could have helped explain Mr. H's one-year experience at West Point, an experience that leads to his characteristic response of anger and indignation when placed in a disadvantageous position in a hierarchy. Although Mr. H claims, "I never fully understood the system at West Point" (63), I conjecture that he was angry because he realized that he came from a different social class from that of other cadets at West Point.

Let me explain my position. Mr. H's first essay, in which he tells his classmates "who he is," includes this statement: "Playing division one basketball was a dream come true when I accepted a basketball scholarship to the United States Military Academy" (Fox 62). That Mr. H's dream was not what he had hoped it would be is seen in his essay in response to *Their Eyes Were Watching God* (written in response to the theme of "ethnicity and language"). It is in this essay that Mr. H's characteristic response to unfair hierarchies appears: "No person is better than me and I am better than no person." Mr. H displays anger because he was unfairly "treated with such prejudices and as a fourth rate human being" by upper-class cadets who had been in his same situation not long before. He insists that all the cadets were the same, the "so-called cream of the crop" (63).

But I am wondering if all the cadets belonged, in Mr. H's words, "in the same race." *Peterson's Competitive Colleges* illustrates exactly who the "cream of the crop" is. Only 14 percent of those who apply to West Point are accepted, and of those, 65 percent come from the top tenth of their high school graduating classes. Students nominated to West Point pay no tuition, yet Mr. H mentions that he accepted a basketball scholarship to the Academy. Might this fact not suggest that Mr. H's academic credentials do not fit those of other West Point cadets? I suspect that Mr. H's experience at West Point may have angered him because he, like Mr. C, Fox's example of a working-class student, discovered that "he was back in the pack" socially or economically. California State, Chico, where Fox's study takes place, is not included in *Peterson's*.

Other similarities between Mr. H. and Mr. C come to mind as well. Fox notes that Mr. C never "denigrates his background," but instead ignores it (85). Mr. H's essays addressing the influence of class are not quoted, but the absence of such consideration leads me to believe that Mr. H ignores his background in these essays, too. Furthermore, both Mr. H and Mr. C see themselves as exemplary, Mr. H as "leader" of his group and Mr. C as "isolated in the special role of advisor, or superior" (61, 83). And both write for the teacher. Fox notes that Mr. H wanted to be "the best among students"; Mr. C sees himself as the "Perfect Student" (69, 80). Neither writer is much concerned with writing for his subgroup, addressing Fox instead, for he can convey the badge of success, an "A" in the course. As Fox explains, Mr. H's perception of himself as a self-motivated individual and his competition for a grade inhibited "careful consideration of a nonevaluating audience's feelings" (70). Furthermore, "he never really concentrated on either understanding or being understood" (114). Mr. C, too, was "relatively unconcerned about the reception of his work by his fellow students" (87). Nor were Mr. H's and Mr. C's responses to Fox's course unusual. Although Fox considers Mr. C's recognition of the effects of his working-class background on his uses of language (in the final analytical essay) as evidence of some success in his approach, he admits that some students "did not even comply with my wishes to examine language politically," and he admits further to being surprised with the "difficulty of truly teaching this course at all" (117).

Recent experiences of John Peavoy, Howard B. Tinberg, and Lazere may help to explain Fox's difficulties in teaching his class. John Peavoy teaches at Scripps College, a selective, expensive women's college where almost all of the students are white and middle class. Peavoy explains that his women students do not think of themselves as belonging to a certain race, class, or gender. For one thing, if they acknowledge the privileges their race or class bestows on them, they call into question the extent to which they can take credit for "their" accomplishments (Fontaine, Peavoy, and Hunter 5). More importantly, they resist identifying themselves as "women," for that would force them to acknowledge that they occupy a disadvantageous position in the world, "that though they define themselves as individuals who just happen to be females, the world defines them as females," thus limiting their future prospects for success (5). As a consequence, Peavoy's students think of themselves as "unique individuals," who by dint of ability and hard work can achieve whatever goals they set for themselves.

Peavoy explains the effects of this vision in his Freshman Humanities Class, which investigates the causes of violence in society. He chooses readings that connect violence with societal inequities. But his students do not make this connection between themselves and violence in society (except, perhaps, as victims of it). As Peavoy maintains, "thinking of yourself as a primarily unique individual works against seeing yourself as a member of a community" (6). Fox's Mr. H and Mr. C seem to me to be very like Peavoy's students. They, too, resisted seeing themselves as limited by class and thought of themselves as unique individuals, thereby thwarting the goal of Fox's pedagogy, to "work against [the] sense of exclusion that many working class, black, and women students feel in education" (90). If Fox's students are like Peavoy's, and I am arguing that they are, these unique individuals will not see any relationship between themselves and the sense of exclusion these groups feel.

Tinberg's students, at Bristol Community College in Fall River, Massachusetts, are light years away from Peavoy's in terms of class and opportunity, but their resistance to seeing themselves as limited by class is similar to Peavoy's students' resistance to seeing themselves as limited by gender. For several years, Fall River has had the state's highest unemployment and high school drop-out rates; furthermore, Tinberg's students come from the "working class," often the first in their families to go to college. They are enrolled, in Tinberg's words, "because they want to find that better job or, more profoundly, to reclaim their self-esteem" (42). Tinberg designed a writing course similar to Fox's, asking his working-class students to reflect on ways "we are shaped or constructed by the culture around us" (41). For one assignment, he asked students to reflect upon ways a classroom-as-culture assigns roles and imposes rules. After reading Freire's "The 'Banking' Concept of Education," the class had no difficulty understanding Freire's message: the "teacher knows everything and students know nothing." The ensuing classroom discussions were lively, filled with students' intense accounts of former instances of powerlessness. But Tinberg was surprised that his students resisted "the *idea* of that powerlessness" (42). It was only in retrospect, when he stepped "outside" his classroom, that he was able to make sense of what had happened. As he explains, the students' responses to Freire's essay were "shaped by, in part, a past powerlessness but also by a persistent belief that they can stem the tide and achieve a measure of control over their lives" (42). "I don't think that anyone can 'make' you play a role that you don't want," declared one young woman (42). Given their backgrounds and their hopes, Tinberg ultimately concludes, his students "could have scarcely reacted otherwise" (42).

Lazere teaches at Cal Poly, San Luis Obispo, an institution not unlike Chico. Lazere describes his students as "middle class economically" (18), just as Fox describes his as "mostly from middle and upper levels of society" (38). But Lazere makes an important distinction that Fox does not, namely, that his students (and I suspect Fox's as well) lack what Pierre Bourdieu terms

> cultural capital—including proficiency in standard English, cultural literacy, and critical understanding of social forces; in other words, their cognitive and linguistic codes are the restricted ones [Basil] Bernstein associates with the working class. ("Back" 18)

(In a more general sense, Henry A. Giroux defines Bourdieu's and Bernstein's concepts of cultural capital as "those systems of meanings, taste, dispositions, attitudes and norms that are directly and indirectly defined by the dominant society as socially legitimate" [*Teachers* 77].) Lazere also challenges his middle-class students in a non-elite college to "examine their conditioned belief in their freedom of choice and mobility within American society by bringing them to a critical con-sciousness of the constrictions in their own class position" ("Back" 18). Although Lazere, like Tinberg, reports that his students react with "initial defensiveness" to the concept that there are "gross inequities between the upper class and themselves," "most students end up affirming the validity of these critical views and start to question their prior educa-tional and vocational choices" (19). Unlike Fox and Tinberg, Lazere offers no detailed examples of students' texts to support his conclusion. Despite Lazere's experience to the contrary, I suspect that Fox's students resisted his pedagogy in much the same way that Tinberg's did his because they did not want to acknowledge "the gross inequities between the upper class and themselves." I suspect as well that Fox's students were trying to acquire the capital that would enable them to join the ranks at the top. For them, the best way to achieve this goal is to distinguish themselves as unique individuals.

In his review of *The Social Uses of Writing*, Gordon P. Thomas notes that he is hesitant to attempt such a radical pedagogy as Fox's, in spite of

> a large mass of language and educational research [that] sup-ports the agenda of radical pedagogy—everything from studies that challenge the "deficit" theories that attempt to explain what is wrong with Black English to revisions of the reproduc-tive theories that explain how schooling perpetuates social class. (222)

I think that all composition teachers, not just those who teach basic writers, must be cautious of adopting these pedagogies as well. In their rush to forestall Hirsch's limited concept of literacy and enable their students to become critically literate, I wonder if compositionists have forgotten that American postsecondary institutions now enroll fully 50 percent of the college-age population, thus increasing the dis-tance between the literacies that students bring with them and that of the traditional college curriculum. Even those students from middle-income families have little connection to bourgeois culture—their extracurricular activities are more likely to involve a job than campus clubs or even sports (Herzberg 115). Additionally, they are not seeking the kinds of literacies that the traditional college curriculum offers. As a consequence of this gap between students' goals and the traditional college curriculum, Richard Ohmann's assertion in his Foreword to *The Politics of Writing Instruction*, that radical pedagogies such as Fox's and Tinberg's have "a good deal more appeal to class-assured students ... than to those ... at the community college" (xiv), seems particularly apt. Moreover, as both Thomas and Villanueva argue, such radical pedagogies do not prepare students for the literacy that they seek.

In order to illustrate the gap between students' desires and those of their teachers, I am recording the responses of two of my "basic writing" students, Mexican Americans, to some questions I asked on opening day of all students who were enrolled in an English A course I taught at the University of Las Vegas, Nevada, last spring. "What goals do you hope to achieve in this class? Please describe these as specifically as possible" I asked on a "Student Data Sheet." Andrés replied, "To improve my writing and English skills. I need to relearn what, I think I missed in high school. To become a better person with my English skills." Ory, who was proud to be the first in his family to graduate from high school, said, "I hope to become a better writer and to understand the skills needed to be successful in life." Our students marginalized by class ask a great deal of literacy and a great deal of us, their instructors, but what pedagogy, radical or not, could impart what Andrés and Ory ask of it?

Pointing out the gap between students' desires and those of their teachers is the easy part. Deciding what to do about this gap is far more difficult. For Bizzell's, Bartholomae's, and Rose's "outsiders," such radical pedagogies are often empowering because competitive colleges and universities have the funds to provide specialists like Mike Rose in their tutoring centers. In other less competitive colleges and universities, as well as in the community colleges, compositionists advocating radical pedagogies may discover that such pedagogies have just the opposite effect of the one that they intend. When faced with the "problem" of class in their situations in society, many of these working-class students (in Lazere's sense of the word) retreat into postures of unique individuals. I am not arguing against radical pedagogy, but I am suggesting that it is far more difficult to implement than compositionists might think and that it can have exactly the opposite effect from the one it is intended to promote, the establishment of a literacy community where people who care about one another converse.

3

Silence(s) in the Academy

> The discourse of academe, whether in writing,
> the classroom, or the meeting, is one of floor-
> holding, not collaborative reciprocity. That, too,
> is characteristically masculine. But writing on
> women's language has come largely out of the
> academy, and is of the academy. We use their
> language to tout ours—a bit schizophrenic.
> —Robin Lakoff

In the last chapter, I looked at basic writing as an important site of the literacy/illiteracy debate, analyzing, in particular, radical pedagogies designed to empower students marginalized by class. As I argued, these pedagogies may well be counterproductive in less competitive postsecondary institutions, for the practical literacy that so many "middle-class" students seek is often at odds with the transformative critical literacy their radical writing teachers seek to impart. In this chapter, I will examine gender as another marginalizing aspect of literacy, paying particular attention to the psychological and sociological premises that underlie the feminist critique of "masculinist" academic discourse conventions. More specifically, I will look at the pedagogies feminist compositionists propose, suggesting that in their isolation of gender as a marginalizing factor, these pedagogies designed to empower women students not only too-narrowly define women's voices but may unintentionally ignore students from non-traditional and non-Western cultures, thereby silencing them.

On the face of things, it would appear that the concerns of both those scholars focusing on basic writers and those focusing on women in the academy would be similar. In truth, they do share similar concerns. David Bleich's "Sexism in Academic Styles of Learning" offers, perhaps, the best expression of these similarities. He states,

> From a feminist perspective, the teaching of language and literacy is always the teaching of language to the dis-enfranchised. The privileged are themselves disenfranchised insofar as they can speak only to themselves and understand few others; the middle class is disenfranchised by the narrow discourse of how to get ahead; the poor are disenfranchised because others will not listen or hear. . . . It is nothing other than sexism when only the language of masculine interests is considered the proper subject in the study of literacy—the language of academic discourse and expository prose. . . . (246)

But there are important differences between these perspectives as well. For one, as Elizabeth A. Flynn notes, the field of composition "has strangely resisted addressing women's issues" ("Composition" 137), while it has displayed a comparatively long and continuing interest in the issue of basic writing. *The Journal of Basic Writing*, for example, was first published in 1975; and the Conference on Basic Writing, a special interest group of the Conference on College Composition and Communication (CCCC), has sponsored National Basic Writing Conferences in 1985, 1987, 1989, and again in 1992. In addition, scholarship focusing on basic writers has been well-received. Mike Rose's *Lives on the Boundary*, described at some length in Chapter 2, received the 1989 David H. Russell Award for Distinguished Research. With the beginning of a new decade, however, feminist scholarship in the field of composition has suddenly blossomed. In 1990, the *Journal of Advanced Composition* published a special issue, "Gender, Culture, and Ideology"; *College English* published two consecutive issues in response to a call for scholarship "devoted to gender-related topics"; and *College Composition and Communication* issued a call for articles on "Gender, Writing, and Pedagogy." Moreover, the 1991 CCCC Convention scheduled a full-day workshop, entitled "Reconsidering Composition Studies from a Feminist Perspective"; Flynn was a presenter.

Differing methodologies also distinguish basic writing scholars' perspectives on composition studies from those of feminist scholars. Mina Shaughnessy's *Errors and Expectations*, still the most important study of basic writers and their prose, is, in Stephen North's taxonomy, an example of "practitioner's lore." Feminist approaches to composition reflect the interdisciplinary nature of feminist studies in general, and while practitioners' stories are valued, forays into other fields provide many of the premises underlying the feminist critique of academic literacy. Barrie Thorne, Cheris Kramarae, and Nancy Henley point out that research on language and gender has been particularly influenced by anthropology, child development, education, folklore, psychology, linguistics, sociology, and speech communications. In addition, drawbacks inherent in practitioner's lore are different from those inherent in an interdisciplinary approach. I discussed one of the major limitations of practitioner's lore in Chapter 2 of this study, namely, a reductive view of basic writers as disempowered lower-class students, a view that derives from the limited experiences of practitioners at just a few isolated institutions. Feminist approaches to composition, on the other hand, are subject to other limitations. North claims that "forays" into other fields—psychology, sociolinguistics, speech communication, for example—can go astray if the foragers consider the premises that they borrow unassailable (102–3). Just this sort of situation has happened in feminist approaches to composition based upon psychological studies. Competition/collaboration, man/woman—the field of psychology is rife with dualisms, dualisms which, in turn, both inform and limit the feminist pedagogy based upon psychological premises (Cooper, "Dueling" 182).

THE FEMINIST CRITIQUE OF ACADEMIC LITERACY

At the conclusion of "Composition Studies from a Feminist Perspective," Flynn suggests that future feminist critiques of composition studies ought to employ two strategies, the identification of androcentrism and the "recuperation" of modes of thinking that are more consistent with "women's ways of knowing," and singles out Bleich's *The Double Perspective* as a model work that employs both strategies (143, 149). Flynn's approbation is one reason why I begin this discussion of the feminist critique with Bleich's *The Double Perspective*, but Bleich's borrowing from Nancy Chodorow and Carol Gilligan in much the same way feminists and feminist compositionists have is another reason. (The most frequently cited works in the articles included in the special gender editions of the *Journal of Advanced Composition* and *College English* are Chodorow's *The Reproduction of Mothering*, Gilligan's *In a Different Voice*, and Mary Field Belenky, Blythe McVicker Clinchy, Nancy Rule Goldberger, and Jill Mattuck Tarule's *Women's Ways of Knowing*.) Finally, Joyce Irene Middleton's and Flynn's assessments of the importance of Bleich's work for compositionists have proved to be prophetic. Several recent studies from a feminist perspective cite Bleich's *The Double Perspective* as an influence (see Kraemer, "No," and Susan Hunter, "Dangers" and "Woman's" as examples).

As described in Chapter 2, Bleich finds that the study of language in the academy, with its "fascination with mystery and paradox" and "its axiomatic use of hierarchical thinking," has been, until recently, androcentric (55, 57). Moreover, he contends that "it would not be an exaggeration to claim that . . . the social psychology of the academy is the social psychology of men functioning among themselves" (5). Bleich draws upon Chodorow's challenge to Freud's notion that a girl's difficulty in breaking her original attachment to her mother is instinctual and Gilligan's studies of the differences in masculine and feminine ways of approaching moral judgments to show how this androcentric bent of academic discourse contrasts with a feminist style of thought that aims for "nonoppositional styles in the study of language and knowledge" (57). All in all, he finds that the student examples of literary response and language use that he includes in his study exhibit "styles consistent with the accounts of child development and gender socialization given by Chodorow and Gilligan," styles that may be "biologically linked, yet not biologically necessary" (122).

Chodorow's examination of "psychoanalysis and the sociology of gender" provides the premises upon which many feminist compositionists base their pedagogies. Madeleine Grumet, in *Bitter Milk*, assesses the value of Chodorow's scholarship in this way:

> Chodorow's schematic presentation of object relations [relations that contain the object of a child's love and thought] is a magnificent contribution to those of us who work to understand the relation of gender to the symbol systems that constitute knowledge, curriculum, and schooling. (11)

Chodorow's study contends that "the psychological processes and the features of gender personality that grow out of the Oedipus complex are grounded in family structure and family development" (159). As she explains, because mothers bear most of the responsibility for early child care,

> Girls' identification processes, then, are more continuously embedded and mediated by their ongoing relationship with their mother. They develop through and stress particularistic and affective relationships to others. A boy's identification processes are not likely to be so embedded in or mediated by a real affective relation to his father. At the same time, he tends to deny identification with and relationship to his mother and reject what he takes to be the feminine world; masculinity is defined as much negatively as positively. Masculine identification processes stress differentiation from others, denial of affective relation, and categorical universalistic components of the masculine role. Feminine identification processes are relational, whereas masculine identification processes tend to deny relationship. (176)

Feminist compositionists draw upon Chodorow's theory of the socially constructed identification processes of women to argue that women's relational processes are at odds with the characteristically masculine "floor-holding" discourse of the academy, whether spoken or written.

Gilligan's *In a Different Voice* extends Chodorow's study and is the most frequently cited work in essays included in the *Journal of Advanced Composition*'s and *College English*'s special issues on gender. Although James N. Laditka acknowledges that Gilligan's oppositional thinking can "lead to overgeneralization and insidious stereotyping," he nonetheless finds Gilligan's research instructive (367). Of interest to feminist compositionists is her account of gender socialization, especially as it points up differences between men's and women's constructions of moral problems. According to Gilligan, women's mode of thinking is "contextual and narrative rather than formal and abstract," and women "make a different sense of experience, based on their knowledge of human relationships" (19, 172). Furthermore, while women's psychology is oriented toward "relationships and interdependence," society's "developmental litany intones the celebration of separation, autonomy, individuation, and natural rights" (22, 23). She concludes by stating that "a recognition of the differences in women's experiences and understanding expands our views of maturity and points to the contextual nature of developmental truths" (174). Gilligan's research supports feminist compositionists' contention that the literate discourse valued by the academy is formal, abstract, individualistic (and, therefore, masculine). Women who are socialized to think narratively and to value attachment rather than separation will find themselves, in Bleich's words, disenfranchised in an academy which values "only the language of masculine interests."

Belenky and her coauthors build upon Gilligan's insights when they offer an alternative perspective to William Perry's *Forms of Intellectual and Ethical Development in the College Years.* Just as Gilligan concludes that women's moral development differs from that of men, Belenky and her colleagues conclude that women's intellectual development differs from that of men as well. Perry's scheme, based on interviews with Harvard men, posits a linear sequence of four epistemological positions: basic dualism, multiplicity, relativism subordinate, and relativism, while *Women's Ways of Knowing*, based on interviews with 135 women, posits five (not necessarily sequential) categories to describe different ways that women construct truth and reality. Belenky and her colleagues describe these epistemological positions as positions of "silence," "received knowledge," "subjective knowledge," "procedural knowledge," and "constructed knowledge." Moreover, they contend that the "authoritarian banking model" of education, described by Paulo Freire, and the "adversarial doubting model," described by Peter Elbow, are "wrong for women" and lead to "alienation, repression, and division," thereby "retarding, arresting, or even reversing [women's] growth" (228). What women need is a "connected model of education" in which "midwife-teachers" help women "develop their authentic voices" through an emphasis on "connection over separation, understanding and acceptance over assessment" and by "according respect to and by allowing time for the knowledge that emerges from firsthand experience" (229).

Women's Ways of Knowing demonstrates the impact of sociolinguistics on feminist scholarship in general, and by extension, on feminist composition theory. The feminist perspective in sociolinguistics generally points out that women have been excluded from research (as in William Labov's studies) or that linguistic features identified as feminine are a reflection of men's dominance and women's subordination. In *Women's Ways of Knowing*, Belenky and her coauthors cite studies by Lakoff, Thorne and Kramarae, and Candace West and Don H. Zimmerman—among the most respected studies in the field—as background for their inquiry. Lakoff's description of women's style of speech in *Language and Women's Place* is so pivotal to the study of language and gender that fellow sociolinguists grant it a place in "folklinguistic lore" (Coates 66) and note that researchers who followed often felt obliged to begin their own research with the "so-called Lakoff hypothesis" (Cameron, McAlinden, and O'Leary 75). The "Lakoff hypothesis" posits a typical female style of speech, one marked by the use of hesitations, intensifiers and qualifiers, tag questions, rising intonation on declaratives, and "empty adjectives"—features which serve to weaken or mitigate the force of an utterance (53). According to Lakoff,

> If a little girl learns her lesson well [that is, if she becomes competent in the female style], she is not rewarded with unquestioned acceptance on the part of society; rather, the acquisition of this special style of speech will later be an excuse others use to keep her in a demeaning position, to refuse to take her seriously as a human being. (qtd. in Coates and Cameron 66)

In her more recent *Talking Power*, Lakoff states that the women's language features she observed in the speech style among members of the North American, educated, white, middle-class community is characteristic of women's language in general, for "language represents behavior supposedly typical of women across the majority of cultures: alleged submissiveness, sexual utility to men, secondary status" (202–3). She also points out an especially important issue for composition scholarship. She claims that women cannot agree on how they should talk: Should women adopt men's language? Should they hold on to open and collaborative language and try to change men's style of speech? Lakoff claims, and the feminist pedagogies that I will examine shortly confirm, that "lately, the thrust has been to the latter" (213).

Other sociolinguistic studies of importance to feminist pedagogies include those by Pamela M. Fishman and West and Zimmerman. Although neither begins with the "Lakoff hypothesis," both demonstrate that socially constructed, hierarchical social relations between men and women are embedded in the stylistic differences in men's and women's language use. After analyzing recorded conversations of three heterosexual couples, Fishman concludes that "there is an unequal distribution of work in conversation." In a description of the division of conversational labor that has become a classic, Fishman decrees that "women are the 'shitworkers' of routine interaction," while men, who do far less interactive work "either control or benefit from the process" (98, 99). West and Zimmerman report the results of a study that investigated patterns of interruptions (violations of speakers' turns at talk) among five men and five women who were first- or second-year university students. Their study showed that more than 90 percent of the interruptions recorded were done by males to females. West and Zimmerman conclude that

> The asymmetry in the initiation of interruption, insofar as it is a stable feature of the verbal interaction between men and women in this society, *constitutes* a powerful differential readily found in both ordinary and extraordinary settings in which men and women come together. (111)

FEMINIST PEDAGOGIES

Composition researchers whose work is collected in Cynthia L. Caywood and Gillian R. Overing's *Teaching Writing: Pedagogy, Gender, and Equity* focus on empowering women students. Several of the twenty essays collected therein cite the same feminist psychologists and sociolinguists that studies printed in the special gender issues of the *Journal of Advanced Composition* and *College English* do (see Annas, Goulston, and Stanger, for example). Since I shall be discussing these journals' special gender issues shortly, I will focus here on "equity" practices set forth in Caywood and Overing's collection, the "recuperative work" of feminism that Flynn calls for. The authors of essay after essay give evidence of Lakoff's claim that women are being advised to hold on to their open and collaborative language rather than to adopt men's styles. Editors Caywood and Overing define feminist pedagogy as a validation of the "private voice" and feminist modes of expression (diaries, freewriting, letters, exploratory essays) associated with it (xiii). Moreover, Wendy Goulston suggests that the use of these "familiar" modes enables women to "draw on their own thinking and feeling to develop the rhetorical strategies that best suit their styles, their arguments, their values" (25–26).

Journals are a favorite and important part of many of the

feminist writing classes described in this collection. Donna M. Perry, who uses journals in her "Women's Changing Roles" course, states that journals give her primarily white, mainly middle-class students "a place in which to write about what for them were taboo subjects (homosexuality, abortion, etc.)" (152). James D. Riemer uses a semester-long journal in his honors composition course to give students an opportunity "to reveal feelings, thoughts, and personal experiences they might have felt uneasy about sharing with the class, particularly if they felt their views went against those expressed in the readings or by other students in class discussions" (159).

Moreover, these feminist compositionists feel that journal writing and feminist pedagogy is appropriate for writing classes in general. As Susan Hunter notes, many of the essays collected in Caywood and Overing's *Teaching Writing* "argue for transforming the composition classroom into a feminist language classroom" ("Woman's" 232). Pamela Annas's "Silences: Feminist Language Research and the Teaching of Writing" is representative of the collection and perhaps the best known essay in the collection. Drawing insights from her work with all-women groups, she argues for feminist discourse in mixed-sex writing courses as well. Likewise, Elisabeth Daumer and Sandra Runzo state that their writing assignments (all of which address women's lives and meanings) can "easily be modified to include men" (47). More importantly, despite Caywood and Overing's caution that their pedagogy "may not meet some of the particular needs of minority students" (xv), several essays in their anthology echo Annas's "Style as Politics: A Feminist Approach to the Teaching of Writing" (the forerunner and source of much of "Silences"), in which she asserts, without a shred of evidence, that much of what she will be saying about the "urban, older, often working-class students" at the University of Massachusetts, Boston, is "adaptable to the teaching of writing to members of other groups disadvantaged in their relation to language" (361). What Annas "is saying here" is that compositionists need to expand the notion of what makes writing good and effective so that it brings together "the personal and the political, the private and the public" and "makes room for the personal voice of experience" (370). I could not agree more with Annas. My concern is with her easy extension of her pedagogy devised for women (and a special group of women at that) to members of other "disadvantaged" disenfranchised groups.

Numerous feminist compositionists have drawn upon the work of feminist psychologists in following Flynn's suggested strategy of pointing out androcentrism in the field of composition studies. Flynn herself and Marilyn M. Cooper, colleagues at Michigan Technological University, were among the first feminist compositionists to respond to Belenky and her colleagues' reconceptualization of the ways women come to know and name their world. Cooper's "Women's Ways of Writing," best described as a reading of *Women's Ways of Knowing*, considers whether "differences in the way women think might motivate different strategies for teaching women to write" (141). Beginning with the observation that some students "do not take well to academic discourse," Cooper concludes with a plea for "midwife teachers" as defined by Belenky and her colleagues (141, 155). One strategy that she recommends for the physically and emotionally abused women upon whom she focuses in this essay is the use of a "computer assisted common journal," a practice that she has employed successfully in first-year writing classes at Michigan Tech as well.

Flynn's "Composing as a Woman," a study of four narratives written by first-year students in which they describe learning experiences, draws upon Chodorow's and Gilligan's scholarship in addition to that of Belenky and her coauthors. Although Flynn defines the authors of the four narratives, two male and two female students, by gender and first name only (Jim, Joe, Kim, and Kathy), the activities that they describe in their narratives—a balloon ride to relieve boredom, a trip to Germany, a solo airplane flight, a father's driving his son forty miles roundtrip to high school swim team practices—strongly suggest that these students are not freshly arrived from the racial or ethnic enclaves of Detroit. The description of Michigan Technological University in *Peterson's Competi-*

tive Colleges supports my contention, for *Peterson's* reports that African American, Native American, Hispanic, and Asian American students each comprise just 1 percent of the total enrollment. (Curiously, international students account for 4 percent of the University's enrollment.) If the first-year writing class that Cooper describes in "Unhappy Consciousness in First-Year English" is representative of first-year writing classes at Michigan Tech, then Flynn's class was probably composed of traditional-age, mostly male students, "planning careers in the creation and implementation of technology" (30, 37). In fact, *Peterson's* reports that Michigan Tech's most popular majors are mechanical engineering, electrical engineering, and civil engineering (170).

Flynn's relative unconcern for the social context of her study is a subject that I shall return to shortly, but first I want to focus on the influences of Chodorow, Gilligan, and Belenky and her colleagues. Declaring that "if women and men differ in their relational capacities and in their moral and intellectual development, we would expect to find manifestations of these differences in the student papers we encounter in our first-year composition courses," Flynn proceeds to discuss the four narratives from a feminist perspective (427–28). She borrows the by-now familiar terminology of the feminist psychologists whose work informs hers and determines that Kim's and Kathy's narratives were characterized by interaction, connection, and frustrated connection, while Jim's and Joe's were characterized by separation, achievement, or frustrated achievement (428). All in all, Flynn suggests that models of the composing process that inform so many pedagogies may well be androcentric and describes an alternative feminist approach to writing that has worked well in her composition classes, a focus on the subject of gender-related differences in behavior and language (432). Such a focus, Flynn posits, "leads [students] toward an understanding of the complexity of interpersonal and social interactions and transactions" and "is bound to help rectify social and political inequities" (Rev. 225).

Like Cooper and Flynn, Don Kraemer and Mary Kupiec Cayton analyze the androcentric bent of academic discourse by drawing upon research by feminist psychologists. Kraemer's "No Exit: A Play of Literacy and Gender" begins with an explanation of the empirical feminist critique of literacy. As he describes it, "for women as for men, writing and reading are institutional practices governed by the same logic that determines social relations at large." It follows, then, that "if women disproportionately suffer the effects of our culture," "women may also suffer disproportionately" in discursive performances (307–8). In addition, Kraemer unpacks Myron Tuman's metaphor of "literacy as game," borrowing extensively from Gilligan and Belenky to do so. He demonstrates that Tuman's version of literacy is a masculine one, resting upon competition, individualism, and abstract thinking—values that run counter to these feminist psychologists' theories of women's moral and intellectual development. Unlike many feminist compositionists, Kraemer does not conclude that composition classrooms must become sites of feminine discourse forms only. On the one hand, he feels that the argumentative structure that the academy values "can prevent both women and men from knowing and changing"; on the other hand, like Flynn, he feels that students gain understanding of one another when they investigate the differences between masculine and feminine approaches to language (316).

Cayton cites Gilligan, Belenky, Flynn, and Cooper in her discussion of gender-specific difficulties women encounter when negotiating the conventions of academic discourse. She explains that "women's location vis-à-vis male-centered discourse communities may lead as a matter of course to nonfunctional or contradictory strategies or paralyzing 'rule rigidity'" ("What" 333). Pointing out differences between men's and women's writing blocks, Cayton notes that men most often wrote about cognitive blocks that they experienced in analyzing issues, while women wrote about the affective blocks that they experienced, either while trying to "connect" with their intended audiences and/or peer writing groups, or while trying to find "authentic voices" in discourse acceptable to the academy. In the end, she reiterates a familiar feminist critique of academic literacy: "To enter into a discourse shaped principally by men's experience and values may leave some women uncomfortable with, even anxious about, some of the ways of thinking it demands" ("What" 333).

A CRITIQUE OF FORAYS INTO PSYCHOLOGY AND SOCIOLINGUISTICS

Feminist compositionists have begun to question uncritical borrowings of feminist psychologists' theories. In their interview with Mary Belenky, for example, Evelyn Ashton-Jones and Dene Kay Thomas suggest to Belenky that research concerned with women only may "reinforce gender stereotypes and essentialist definitions of femininity" (284). In her response to the interview, Flynn acknowledges that Belenky's work is valuable to compositionists in its concentration on the long-neglected ways women learn. But, in pointing out the ways Belenky and her coauthors have used the work of Chodorow—that is, "to emphasize the connectedness of mother and daughter and, by implication, the connectedness of woman to woman"—she demurs, arguing that both her own experiences and her readings of other feminists convince her that Belenky and her colleagues' "very positive portrayal" of the community of women and the implication that men are responsible for barriers to women's development is far too simplistic ("Politicizing" 176). She agrees instead with Evelyn Fox Keller and Helene Moglen's conclusion that "conflict and competition are inescapable facts of both inner and outer realities of women's lives," and that it is better to acknowledge the fact than to deny it (qtd. in Flynn 177).

In another response to Ashton-Jones and Thomas's interview with Belenky, Marilyn Cooper argues that Belenky and her coauthors' work exhibits the same competition/collaborative, man/woman, and cognitive/social dualisms that underlie the field of psychology in general. As a consequence of these dualistic conceptions, Cooper maintains that in Belenky's work women "are excluded from reasoned critical discourse" and that their cognitive perspective relegates "social context to an addendum" ("Dueling" 180, 183). In addition, Black feminist Patricia Hill Collins, while crediting Chodorow's and Gilligan's significant contributions to feminist theory, points out that the absence of Black feminist ideas from their studies severely limits them (7–8). Meryl Altman turns a critical eye on the metaphors of maternity and mothering that inform so many literary studies, arguing that they push class, age, and race differences within "woman" to the margins (501). She attributes the "disturbing centrality" of these metaphors in the discourse to the influence of Gilligan and Chodorow, whose empirical studies seem "real-er" to English majors (501, 502). Importantly, these same metaphors are so much a part of the fabric of "Women's Ways of Writing," Daumer and Runzo's study, and Catherine E. Lamb's "Beyond Argument in Feminist Composition" that compositionists would do well to question whose voices are suppressed there as well.

Lamb also reiterates some of these same concerns. "Current discussion of feminist approaches to teaching composition emphasizes the writer's ability to find her own voice through open-ended, exploratory, often autobiographical, writing," she states, but a feminist theory of composition needs to include argument as well as open-ended, exploratory writing. Lamb recommends negotiation and mediation as approaches that are compatible with "the emphasis on co-operation, collaboration, shared leadership, and integration of the cognitive and affective which is characteristic of feminist pedagogy" (11).

The feminist perspective is relatively new in the field of sociolinguistics, says Flynn ("Composition" 138). Although this perspective has fast taken firm roots, feminist compositionists have just begun to take advantage of its insights (see, for example, Ashton-Jones as well as Kraemer, "Enthymemes"). Critiques of the scholarship of Lakoff, Fishman, and West and Zimmerman more often come from other scholars in the field than from compositionists, whether of feminist bent or not. Coates's reservations about sociolinguists' studies echo the reservations that Cooper has about the field of psychology in general. Assessing studies of colleagues who argue that men's conversational styles are competitive whereas women's are cooperative, Coates points out that their scholarship focuses almost exclusively on white, middle-class, English-speaking women. "We must turn our attention to girls and older women, to working class women, to women from different occupational groups," she says (70, 73). Marsha Houston (Stanback) emphatically agrees:

> Middle-class, mid-Western, white, college sophomores are a limited sample of communicators; no matter how vast their numbers or how sophisticated the analysis of the data they provide, they cannot tell us all that we need to know about human communication. (29–30)

While affirming the essential value of feminist theory as "the only explanatory frame that accounts for women's place in the social order," she cautions that exclusion of Black women from women's studies in communication "perpetuates the myth that women's communication experiences are the same in every social and ethnic group" (28).

Moreover, two recent studies go against the grain of the feminist studies described earlier. Joan Swann, for one, challenges the conclusions that both Fishman's and Zimmerman and West's studies draw about male dominance in mixed-sex conversations. Her observations of classroom interactions in two British elementary schools lead her to conclude that speaking of boys' "dominating" classroom talk oversimplifies things (139). Hesitant as I am about drawing comparisons between college and elementary school classrooms, I feel that Swann's conclusion, that "everyone is an accomplice in the tendency by boys to contribute more to classroom talk—girls too by, arguably, using the resources available in the interactions to contribute less," bears consideration (139). At the very least, her study's demonstration of male dominance of classroom conversation (and female complicity in the arrangement) in elementary school classrooms calls into question how successful a restructured, semester-long feminist classroom can be in changing longstanding social relations perceived as "normal."

A second study calls for a reassessment of Lakoff's notion of women as "conversational facilitators." Again maintaining that linguistic studies ignore context, Cameron, McAlinden, and O'Leary argue that the use of particular linguistic forms may be explained by a number of variables, including gender. For example, women's more frequent use of "tag questions" could be a mark of women's coping with or resistance to conditions of their oppression rather than as a mark of their being responsible for the "interactional shitwork" of conversation (91–92). On a final note, however, in one of the few studies to investigate the interaction of occupational status and gender in mixed-sex conversations, Nicola Woods reports that when these two conflicting power bases are at work, then gender has "the stronger and overriding effect upon floor apportionment" (156). But the study also calls for additional research; in particular, it calls for an investigation into the supporting roles that women play in men's dominance of conversation (157).

Young though the field of feminist composition may be, the first steps of a critique are already in place. One can begin to hear the echoes of the cautions voiced by the sociolinguists above. Mary Kupiec Cayton, for instance, admits that the "population of the students I studied—both men and women—were nearly all white and upper-middle class." In retrospect, she wonders how "value dilemmas" of the Black students in the course differed from those of students marginalized solely by gender. She concludes:

> Research by neither the cognitive nor affective schools has captured the roles that race, class, or other marginalizing factors may play in making writers uneasy with the identity construction required by academic discourse and in blocking their writing altogether. ("What" 334–35)

Cooper's critique of the dualisms that underpin so much psychological research on women is beginning to be heard as well about feminist pedagogies. Kraemer repeats Lamb's concerns that such feminist pedagogies as advocated in Caywood and Overing's collection are reductive in their rejection of logic and argument as inherently masculine ("Enthymemes"

38). Furthermore, in direct response to Flynn's, Cooper's, and Annas's calls for feminist approaches to composition outlined earlier, Susan Hunter forcefully declares that the "proposition that women have been socially constructed to learn better with feminist/composition pedagogy and men with current-traditional pedagogy is reductionist" and has "yet to acknowledge the cognitive and political complexities" of writing classrooms populated by men and women and "culturally different ones" who feel "at home in the academy" ("Woman's" 236, 230–31). Moreover, both Donald Stewart and Ashton-Jones question the uncritical enthusiasm so many feminist compositionists have for collaborative learning. On the one hand, Stewart will grant that it is "a productive alternative for *some* people, primarily extroverts" (496); on the other hand, Ashton-Jones, citing Fishman's and West and Zimmerman's studies, raises serious concerns about the "pedagogy of 'equity' that collaborative learning purports to be." Not only does collaborative learning reveal "a very real and potentially invidious male bias," she argues, but feminist compositionists in their uncritical acceptance of it may unwittingly "teach women a limited subject position from which to write" and "to accept their subordinate place in the social hierarchy of gender" (22, 30).

EXTENDING THE FEMINIST CRITIQUE

I suggested at the beginning of this chapter that when feminist compositionists make forays into feminist psychology for premises upon which to base their pedagogies, the dualisms that underlie feminist psychology become part of the fabric of feminist pedagogy as well. While Kraemer and Lamb and Cooper have already begun a critique of the collaborative/competitive dualism that underlies feminist pedagogy, I want to focus on the cognitive/social dualism that Cooper treats briefly in her response to Ashton-Jones and Thomas's interview with Belenky. Just as Cooper is "infuriated" at the short shrift Belenky gives social context in her studies ("Dueling" 183), so, too, am I uncomfortable with a similar unconcern for social context in the scholarship of so many feminist compositionists. I find that as feminist compositionists seek out and identify incidences of androcentrism in academic discourse, they have more or less ignored the Eurocentric nature of that discourse. As a consequence of this shortsightedness, I am afraid that in a rush to make room for women's voices in the discourse of the academy, compositionists may unintentionally silence basic writers and students from non-Western cultures.

A case in point is Flynn's "Composing as a Woman." I noted earlier that Flynn ignores the social context of her study. Students' description of their personal experiences, Cooper's description of a similar writing class at the same university, and *Peterson's* profile of students enrolled at Michigan Technological University suggest that the class is composed of traditional-age, mostly white, mostly middle-class students. Flynn's students seem not unlike those enrolled at William Paterson, the state college in New Jersey where Perry teaches her women's studies course, but they bear little resemblance to classes of students that I have taught in community colleges, where traditional-age, full-time students majoring in anything other than vocational programs are a rarity. Nor do I suspect that Flynn's and Perry's classrooms much resemble the one that Terry Dean chronicles in "Multicultural Classrooms, Monocultural Teachers." Dean describes his students at the highly competitive University of California, Davis, as "Thai, Cambodian, Vietnamese, Korean, Chinese, Hmong, Laotian (mid-Lao, lowland Lao), Salvadoran, Afro-American, Mexican, French, Chicano, Nicaraguan, Guatemalan, Native American (Patwin, Yurok, Hoopa, Wintu), Indian (Gujarati, Bengali, Punjabi), Mexican-American, Jamaican, Filipino (Tagalog, Visayan, Ilocano), Guamanian, Samoan, and so on" (23). I am suggesting that differences in these classrooms make all of the difference in adopting feminist pedagogies successfully. Flynn has already argued that the "problem of women's silence [is] very complex and the solutions to the problem equally complex" ("Politicizing" 178). I am suggesting that as writing classrooms become increasingly multicultural, the problem of silence and solutions to it are even more complex than feminist compositionists have so far realized. For the remainder of this chapter, I shall underscore difficulties that women marginalized by class as well as by gender may have with writing assignments considered "feminist." In the next chapter, I will develop at length the cultural dissonance that can occur in feminist writing classrooms.

Most of the feminist compositionists who argue for open-ended writing assignments and collaborative learning in writing classrooms have not considered that these feminist modes of expression and learning may be inappropriate for women marginalized by class as well as by gender. Their oversight may well be a consequence of their being situated in mainly white, mainly middle-class institutions. Barbara Henning sounds almost as angry as Cooper when she discusses what can happen to socially excluded students in search of their "inner voices." She contends that personal writing "might well work for the student already safely situated, the student whose education serves as a sweet sixteen introduction to a world full of promise" (680). But for poor students, trying to sustain a personal voice may result in their feeling impotent to change things. In direct counter to the claims of Annas, Henning charges that "no matter how open" methods of teaching purport to be, "many of these approaches rest on assumptions about reality that exclude the non-traditional student." As an example, she offers the experience of a student who had to drop out of school when her funds ran out. "This woman does not need to find an inner voice. . . . This woman needs a paycheck and a babysitter," contends Henning (681).

Nor do I find that it takes much imagination to understand why personal narratives, such as those Flynn describes having her students write in "Composing as a Woman," are uncomfortable for such students as Henning describes. Think, for a moment, what it might be like for such a student to share her learning experience with someone who takes balloon rides when she gets bored or visits Germany on a class trip. In *Lives on the Boundary*, Rose recounts the reaction of Denise, a Hispanic student, to an assignment in her composition class that required her to write about hardships that current immigrants face. He suggested that she write about the ways Hispanic immigrants were treated in Southern California. The exchange that ensued between them is worth quoting:

> She looked at me as though I'd whispered something obscene in her ear. "No!" she said emphatically, pulling back her head, "that's rude." "Rude," I said. "Explain to me what's—" She cut in. "You don't want to put that in a paper. That doesn't belong." Some things were better left unsaid (179).

Instead of narrative freeing Denise from the bonds of academic discourse, the thought of dredging up an ugly past stopped Denise's writing cold (179). As Cayton argues, feminist studies such as hers have not considered the roles that race and class may play in blocking students' writing altogether.

All in all, I am not suggesting that the scholarship of feminist compositionists is wrongheaded or that feminist compositionists should forgo forays into the scholarship of other fields; I have made enough forays of my own in this chapter. What I am suggesting is that we compositionists must be more alert to the cognitive bias of the many studies we find informative and that we must pay more attention to the intersection of race, class, and gender, as Collins, Houston, and Thorne, Kramarae, and Henley suggest. These political categories must and do combine in almost every instance, but it is difficult to predict, in everyday life and in classroom situations, the self-presentation of gender, race, and class identities.

By way of example, consider Linda Brodkey's "On the Subjects of Class and Gender in 'The Literacy Letters,'" to me, one of the most sensitive studies in the field. Despite the "and" in her title, Brodkey considers class *or* gender in two of her three examples (as did Thomas Fox in *The Social Uses of Writing*). As a result, she misses an important intersection of gender and class, an intersection that studies in sociolinguistics might help to explain. Brodkey sets out to investigate the ways discourse constructs our teaching. She examines the personal letters that six middle-class white teachers (four women and two men) exchanged with six white working-class women enrolled in a basic writing class. At the end, Brodkey concludes that the three teacher/student pairs whose letters she details at length lost all opportunity to challenge the ideology of class present in the classroom because the teachers tried to treat the class differences as irrelevant. Of special interest here is Brodkey's discussion of the correspondence between the pair she calls "Don and Dora." She interprets their correspondence from the perspective of differences in class: Don, the teacher/narrator, is in the position of power, whereas Dora, the student/audience, is acted upon (132).

However, I suspect the politics of gender plays an important role in their correspondence as well. Brodkey's descriptions of Don's correspondence—his selection of all the topics, his failure to respond to Dora's topic selections—sound like behaviors Fishman describes in her study of male/female gender relations. Moreover, they resemble the responses of five male instructors in a recent study of gender as a factor in teachers' responses to students' writing. The men read the student papers in the same way men interacted in Fishman's study of cross-gender conversations: they withheld support by concentrating on errors that needed to be fixed, took an authoritarian stance, thereby controlling their students' papers, and raised new topics rather than responding in ways that would encourage students to develop their own (McCracken, Miller, Green, and Greenwood (360, 371). Thus, even if the class differences between the teacher and the student were acknowledged, it is likely that the same hierarchy would still be in play. In fact, as Nicola Woods found, when the power bases of class and gender intersect, gender is the more powerful variable (156).

All in all, I am suggesting that feminist compositionists must recognize the man/woman, competitive/cooperative, cognitive/social dualisms that underpin the fields of psychology and sociolinguists from which they have aptly borrowed so many of their premises. In doing so, I feel that compositionists will not only become more alert to the social contexts of their own increasingly diverse classrooms but will become more aware of the social contexts of the influential feminist studies that they look to for pedagogies to adopt. Michael Holzman tells us that above all, "we must try not to do harm" (138). I cannot think of a teacher who would disagree with him. However, as the next chapter will show, if we fail to consider the intersections of class, gender, and culture, we can unintentionally cause non-mainstream, non-Western students a great deal of discomfort, if not indeed harm.

4

Culture and the Discourse of the Academy

An example of a distortion (or perhaps merely
an oversimplification) of a liberatory principle
appears in the idea of adding previously silenced
voices—of making student, Asian, gay, female,
poor, etc. voices heard. Each voice within these
voices, however, is also a plurality—and not
necessarily a harmonious plurality at that.
There is great intra-individual conflict among
the voices people internalize from a stratified
society. . . . Attempting to merely add voices. . .
ignores the contradictory, partial, "teeth-
gritting" nature of each voice.
— Carole Edelsky

All language use is "interested" and all language instruction is political. But there is a tremendous difference between
examining language use and instruction in relation to the
politics of class and gender and examining language use and
instruction in relation to the politics of culture. When the
literacy/illiteracy debate focuses on culture, the debate
becomes more public, more political, and more polemical.
The stark backdrop of this debate, described by Ernest R.
House, Carol Emmer, and Nancy Lawrence earlier, is worth
repeating here:

> The deteriorating economic condition of the United States, the
> development of a seemingly permanent underclass, and the
> entry of vast numbers of non-English speaking immigrants,
> legal and illegal, have created a situation in which many
> Americans feel threatened. . . . In addition, there is a pervasive
> sense of unease about the United States's slipping economi-
> cally, as reflected in rising trade deficits and a stagnant
> standard of living. (72)

Carole Edelsky adds that "these are terrible times" and that
people who feel impotent in the fact of "horrendous (and
horrendously entwined)" economic, political, and social problems, in a case of "classic displacement, substitute what is
amenable to relatively immediate blame or control for what
is not. And among all public domains, it is education that is
imminently controllable" (155). "After all," queries Edelsky,
"if the United States imports more Toyotas than it exports
Chevrolets, it *must* be the kindergarten teacher's fault,
right?!" (154).

Since Edelsky's remarks were published, other events
have occurred to add to the uneasiness that Americans
feel about their country's economic health and have fueled
anti-Asian and racist sentiments in the bargain. Just before
Christmas 1991, General Motors joined a growing number
of American companies announcing plans to downsize in a
"global economy"; General Motors Chairman Robert C.
Stempel announced plant closings and the permanent elimi-
nation of more than 70,000 jobs. That same month,
International Business Machines unveiled a reorganization
plan designed to enhance its growth; it included the elimina-
tion of more than 40,000 jobs (Wolk). In early 1993, Sears,
Roebuck, and Co. announced a "long-awaited" decision to
exit the catalog business, thereby eliminating 4,300 full-time
and 4,600 part-time positions (Hood and Pilotis 5). While Wall
Street analysts cheered General Motors' restructuring (by
mid-1993, Prudential Securities had upgraded its stock to
"Single Best Idea Status" [Fricke and Shand 1]), the great-great
grandchildren of those immigrants whose presence had led to

the establishment of the American public education system grew fearful that their children, for the first time in American history, would not equal, let alone surpass, their parents' standard of living.

A growing anti-Asian sentiment and racial unrest have further complicated the picture. In early January 1992, following President Bush's four-day visit to Japan with top automobile executives in tow, Yoshio Sakurauchi, speaker of Japan's House of Representatives, expressed the widely held (if seldom openly stated) Japanese opinion of American workers and their products. Sakurauchi placed the blame for the $4.1 billion trade deficit with Japan (automobiles and automobile parts made up 75 percent of that deficit) on lazy American laborers and inferior products. Moreover, he told reporters that the United States would be "judged as finished by the world" if it did not improve worker productivity and product quality (Watanabe 1).

Not surprisingly, some angered Americans responded with scattered incidents of violence directed at Japanese Americans and with "Buy American" campaigns, replete with "patriotic" tee-shirts and Japanese-car-smashing parties—all duly recorded in newspaper headlines and by nightly news videojournalism.

It is in this larger political, social, and economic context that literacy/illiteracy debates concerned with race and ethnicity as marginalizing factors take place. As in the past, literacy is offered as a solution to economic and social problems in the United States. Cultural literacy, especially as defined by E. D. Hirsch Jr., is one favorite solution of government officials. Hirsch's scheme is attractive to government officials and the general public alike because it is short-term, and it places the responsibility for acquiring literacy—a cultural vocabulary—on students and their teachers. Furthermore, the bits of information that Hirsch equates· with literacy can then be measured by national standardized tests.

Chester E. Finn, perhaps Hirsch's most vocal supporter, shows how tests can be used to exclude students who don't measure up. He claims that

The single most potent boost that could be given to student learning in the United States in the 1990s would be for all of our colleges and universities to stand in phalanx and inform schools that they intend to go out of the business of remedial secondary (and primary) education and therefore that, beginning on a specific future date, none will enroll any applicant who does not possess at least "the following skills and knowledge" [as demonstrated by their performances on national tests]. (303)

Furthermore, he proposes that colleges lower tuition rates for students of demonstrated "merit," while denying degree credit and federal and state student-aid funds for remedial courses (304–5). Who will be excluded in Finn's scheme? Pamela Keating and Jeannie Oakes in "Access to Knowledge: Breaking Down School Barriers to Learning" provide an answer:

- The quality of education children receive can be predicted— to a considerable degree—by their race. Black, Hispanic and other non-Asian minorities will not receive equal or high-quality opportunities in schools.
- The quality of education children receive can be predicted— to a considerable degree—by their parents' income. . . .
- The quality of education a child receives can be predicted— to a considerable degree—by his or her gender. . . .
- Classifications [of students] according to ability often reflect language and cultural diversity rather than actual differences in capacity. (qtd. in Stuckey 105)

Hirsch's scheme is anathema to such scholars as Henry Giroux, Patricia Bizzell, Mike Rose, and a minority of members of the National Council of Teachers of English. Giroux claims that Hirsch's notion of literacy "reads more like a phone book list" and that his pedagogy is "profoundly reactionary" and "can be summed up in the terms 'transmission' and 'imposition.'" Furthermore, he contends that Hirsch's vision (and Allan Bloom's and Mortimer Adler's as well) is "based on a view of excellence and learning that privileges the white, male, middle class and ignores everyone else" (*Schooling* 118, 120). Mincing no words, he charges,

This is the totalizing discourse of totalitarianism parading behind the veil of cultural restoration. Its enemy is democracy, utopianism, and the unrealized political possibilities contained in the cultures of "the other," that is, those who are poor, black, women, and who share the experience of powerlessness. (120)

Finn minces no words either when he comments upon those who share Giroux's views. In his latest book, Finn recounts the following anecdote as evidence that "our children are in the hands of oddballs" (206). At a gathering of the Educational Commission of the States in 1990, he says that as the moderator introduced him as a panelist, he was hissed by some people at the back of the hall. "A friend remarked later that their name tags identified them as officials of the National Council of Teachers of English (NCTE), a group that from time to time has quarreled with my views on core curricula and student assessment" (218). As for Giroux in particular, Finn associates his conception of education with "far-left politics, the distaste for dominant trends in society, the passion for particularistic multiculturalism and outré life styles, the contempt for authority, and the sheer unreality of so much that appears" in issues of *Harvard Educational Review*. In fact, for Finn, Giroux's theories bring back memories of "Joan Baez, sandal-shod stained-glass makers in Vermont, and upper-middle-class youths going 'underground' after blowing up something for ideological reasons" (226–27). As I said, the debate is not friendly.

Such, then, is the larger context in which debates about definitions of literacy and access to higher education take place, and compositionists, like it or not, are at the forefront of that debate. As American classrooms grow increasingly multiculturally diverse, debates about literacy and access will grow increasingly complex, and the outcomes will have enormous consequences for our students. Teaching multiculturally diverse classes will require compositionists to do more than merely celebrate cultural differences by adding previously silenced voices to classroom conversations. It requires compositionists to become acquainted with the many different literacies these students will be bringing to the classroom. "Very specifically," says sociolinguist Guadalupe Valdés, "teaching non-English-background students must be based on a deep understanding of the nature of societal bilingualism and on the examination of existing views about writing and the development of writing for bilingual writers" (86).

However, the understanding Valdés argues for will be difficult for compositionists to attain. For one thing, as Valdés herself points out, the situation is complicated by "compartmentalization" within the field of composition studies. (Valdés suggests that one compare the membership rolls of the National Council of Teachers of English and Conference on College Composition and Communication with those of Teachers of English to Speakers of Other Languages and National Association of Bilingual Education [88].) As she argues, composition scholarship has focused either on mainstream English-speaking students or students not yet fully functional in English, ignoring the problems of fluent/functional bilinguals. Moreover, she claims, this limited focus "results in a view of the nature of writing and the teaching of composition that can be potentially harmful to a large segment of the population of this country" (89). For another, Alastair Pennycook contends that the views about writing for bilingual writers in the field of English as a Second Language (ESL) are purposely distorted. He charges that the field of ESL, in order to "preserve the status quo" (threatened as it is by the number of Spanish-speaking people in the United States), ignores the "overwhelmingly consistent pattern in the research data showing the efficacy of bilingual programs" because acknowledging them would "effectively eliminate the psychoeducational legitimatization for eradicating minority children's language and culture" (503).

This situation concerns me. As we compositionists attempt to deal with our changing classrooms, I am afraid that the pedagogies we adopt, based as they may be on "seriously outdated and inaccurate" characteristics of the student population (Valdés 87), may cause such cultural dissonance that students from non-mainstream cultures will drop out.[5] In particular, I am concerned that feminist pedagogies will be uncritically adopted to teach writing in multicultural class-rooms. More specifically, I am concerned that the adoption of feminist pedagogies, designed to empower women students by means of collaborative and cooperative approaches, may either silence students from other cultures and/or lead to misunderstandings between students from different cultures, especially in collaborative peer writing groups.

THE FACE OF THINGS TO COME

Problems of language use and language instruction in multiculturally diverse classrooms are almost unbeliev-ably complex. To begin to explain this complexity by way of examples, I turn to descriptions of writing classrooms a continent apart. Describing the students in her four Develop-mental Writing classes at the City University of New York in the fall of 1980, Lynn Troyka states that they or their parents were from "Italy, Greece, Yugoslavia, Austria, China, India, Pakistan, Haiti, Jamaica, Barbados, Trinidad, Puerto Rico, Ecuador, Colombia, Nicaragua, Cuba, and America" ("Per-spectives" 253). A decade later and some three-thousand miles away, Stanford University reflects the diversity of Terry Dean's classrooms at the University of California, Davis. Twenty-eight percent of its 13,000 students are members of minority groups; 14 percent are Asian American, the largest segment of the university's minority enrollment (Edwards 15). Nor are such classrooms a phenomenon at coastal univer-sities only. In the fall of 1991, I, too, was surprised at (and unprepared for) the many cultures reflected in the twenty faces sitting before me in a second-semester first-year writing course at the University of Nevada, Las Vegas. Among the students enrolled in that class were: one Indian; one Native American (a Navajo who had grown up on a reservation in Arizona); one Mexican American; two brothers from Canada who conversed in French with one another and in English with the rest of us; two African Americans (a young man from Ithaca, New York, and a returning student, a single mother, from Los Angeles); and a traditional-age Filipino woman who would probably be surprised to find that I had thought to include her in this list at all.

This almost epic catalog of national origins only scratches the surface of the complexity of the problem, however. To begin to describe this situation in more detail, I turn to Jay Robinson's comments in "The Wall of Babel; Or, Up Against the Language Barrier." As Robinson notes, conservative reports derived from the 1960 census indicated that at that time almost ten million white American-born individuals had a language other than English as their first language; in fact, about half of those individuals were children of parents who were born in the United States (56). In a footnote to the essay, republished in *Conversations on the Written Word*, Robinson updates these figures in order to highlight the growing complexity of American multicultural diversity. Drawing upon a 1988 report entitled *New Voices*, he points out that recent patterns of immigration have brought an increasingly large percentage of immigrants from Asian countries; importantly, the structures of their native languages have little relation to English sentence structure, and their systems of writing, unlike those of immigrants from European countries a century ago, do not use the Roman alphabet. Just as one cannot assume that individuals born in the United States speak English as their first language, neither can one assume that these Asian immigrants are not literate in English. Again citing *New Voices*, Robinson claims that 65 percent of Vietnamese immigrants, 44 percent of Laotian immigrants, and 38 percent of Cambodians are literate in English (87).

Surprising as these facts may be to compositionists, this situation is further complicated by compartmentalization within the field of composition studies, resulting in a limited focus on students not yet fluent in English, thereby ignoring the problems of fluent/functional bilinguals. Min-zhan Lu's experience as a student fluent in both Chinese and English is instructive. She substantiates Edelsky's observations when she describes her experience in China, stating that "despite my parents' and teachers' attempts to keep home and school discrete, the internal conflict between discourses continued

whenever I read or wrote" ("From" 445). Turning her attention to the writing classrooms in the United States, she is
concerned with the way "some composition classes focus
on turning the classroom into a monological scene for the
student's reading and writing," for, she argues, it was precisely this separation of home discourse (English) from the
school discourse (Chinese) that prevented her from using the
"interaction" between her discourses constructively. Drawing upon her experience as a fluent/functional bilingual,
Lu maintains that students are "actors" in a "complex and
dynamic social and historical scene beyond the classroom"
and that "we need to call attention to voices that seem
irrelevant to the discourse we teach rather than encourage
them to shut them out" ("From" 447). Finally, in language
that echoes that of Valdés, she states, "When I think of the
ways in which the teaching of reading and writing as classroom activities can frustrate the development of students, I
am almost grateful for [my circumstances in China]." She
feels that the complexity of this experience kept her "from
losing sight of the effort and choice involved in reading or
writing with or through a discourse" ("From" 447).

Unaware of the complexity of multicultural classrooms
and unprepared for the difficulties in implementing solutions
to the silence of minority voices, compositionists, ready or
not, can expect to face increasingly diverse writing classrooms. By way of example, Robinson cites demographic
projections published in *Education Week* in 1986 to demonstrate that by the year 2000, "thirty-eight percent of the under
eighteen population will be black, Asian, Native American,
and Hispanic" ("Wall" 86). This increasingly diverse population is already showing up in postsecondary institutions.
According to the *Tenth Annual Status Report on Minorities
in Higher Education (1991)*, while white student enrollment
rose by 3.8 percent nationwide, that of Asian students
increased by 11.7 percent. Native American student enrollment increased by 10.8 percent during this same period,
Hispanic enrollment grew 11.5 percent, and African American enrollment increased by 8.2 percent (American 11–13).
All in all, from 1988 to 1990, the numbers of minority stu-

dents in higher education rose by 10 percent (1). Furthermore, enrollment of foreign students in American colleges and universities has increased dramatically as well. A recent article in the *Chronicle of Higher Education* reports that in the last thirty years, foreign student enrollment in U.S. colleges has increased almost eightfold, from a little more than 53,000 students in the 1960–1961 academic year to more than 450,000 students in the 1990–1991 academic year. Importantly, more than half of the foreign students enrolled in 1990–1991 came from Asian countries. In fact, their percentage of the total foreign enrollment has increased from just under 38 percent thirty years ago to more than 56 percent today. The *Chronicle* further reports that in 1990–1991, the largest number of foreign students came from China; the next largest numbers came from Japan, Taiwan, India, and the Republic of Korea ("Foreign" A1, A30).

Although statistics never tell a complete story, the concurrence of report after report indicates that American college campuses are becoming increasingly ethnically diverse. Moreover, as Valdés notes, "For English composition professionals, working effectively with diverse students will require extensive knowledge about this new minority population" (86), knowledge that our limited research does not provide.

FEMINIST PEDAGOGY IN MULTICULTURAL CLASSROOMS

Although the different languages that students bring with them to writing classes may be enough to daunt many composition teachers, such differences represent just one part of the different literacies that students bring to class. Differences in the rhetorical traditions of these different languages may be just as perplexing, and because of the similarities between Asian and Eastern rhetorics and language associated with women's ways of writing, these differences may be overlooked. To explain this confusing situation better, let me first point out similar features of language use labeled "Asian" or "Eastern" and that associated with "feminine" discourse.

By way of a brief review, feminist pedagogy emphasizes cooperation, collaboration, and shared leadership (Lamb 11). The role of the teacher in such a pedagogy is that of "mid-wife—she "must be a 'benign authority,' an ally, a confidante, an equal who cares for her students and believes they know something and have a voice" (Cooper, "Women's" 156). Furthermore, feminist approaches to teaching writing emphasize "open-ended, exploratory, often autobiographical, writing" (Lamb 11), an emphasis largely at odds with the predominant model of academic literacy which is centered on the "values of competition and individualization" (Kraemer, "No" 310). When women adopt this distinctive register of academic discourse, many feel a "loss of confidence, connection, [and] comfort" (311). In order to obviate these difficulties women encounter in the discourse of the academy, feminist compositionists advocate a supportive and critical classroom, one that permits both experimental and expository prose, one where students work in small groups critiquing one another's writing (Annas, "Silences" 14).

A reading of several recent essays focusing on Eastern/ Asian rhetorics points out the similarities between these rhetorics and women's approaches to discourse.[6] Carolyn Matalene, for one, reiterates the by now familiar dictum that Western Aristotelian rhetorical standards are "expressions of Western culture, applicable within the context of Western cultural values" and, therefore, are not universal. Citing Robert Oliver's *Communication and Culture in Ancient India and China*, Matalene hypothesizes that "a culture's rhetoric constitutes an interface where the prescriptions of language meet the practices of culture" (789, 790). Furthermore, she sounds rather like Bleich when she contrasts Western rhetoric, an "arena for combatants" that provides an "avenue for the individual to achieve control by saying something new in a new way," with Chinese rhetoric, a site of "harmony" that seeks to promote "social cohesion" by appealing to history and tradition and by always repeating "maxims, examples, and analogies presented in the established forms and well-known phrases" (795). "Eastern" rhetoric may be further characterized, she notes, by the

"delayed argument followed by a turn, and the final unconnected assertions" (801). For example, she notes that the
practice of citing references is one consistent with Western
culture's emphasis on individualism, while the Chinese practice of repetition and imitation is consistent with a culture
that values the "harmony of the group" (803, 804).

LuMing Mao reiterates many of Matalene's points in
another recent essay. Again, in almost Bleichean terms, she
insists that the tradition of Western persuasive discourse is an
"agonistic discourse, forever situated in a confrontational
context" (132). Drawing upon James Kinneavy's *A Theory of
Discourse: The Aims of Discourse* and Richard Ohmann's "In
Lieu of a New Rhetoric," she asserts that Western traditional
rhetoric presumes an oppositional audience and a writer
whose purpose it is to overcome this audience's objections
(134). Likewise drawing upon Oliver, Mao repeats Matalene's
point that Western rhetoric is antithetical to Chinese and
Indian rhetorics (and to Japanese, too, she adds) because
Chinese and Indian rhetorics "stress the need to avoid any
appearance of clash of opinion and highlight the importance
of achieving harmony and unity as the objectives of their
discourse" (136). Student writing informed by "this kind of
non-confrontational rhetoric," claims Mao, "will certainly be
considered inadequate or outright improper simply because
it is either a 'deviation' from the 'norm' or believed to be
ineffective in achieving its objectives" (137). She cites Paul
Grice's cooperative model of conversation and Kenneth
Burke's concept of identification in order to propose a new
model of persuasive discourse, one based on cooperation
through identification (131, 137). Turning from theory to
practice, Mao contends that rhetoric textbooks and writing
classrooms should make room for a persuasive discourse of
cooperation while retaining the traditional Western model
of oppositional rhetoric (137). As a consequence of this shift of
emphasis in writing classrooms, "everyone in this process,
which is equally cooperative, will reap a sense of empowerment and of the importance of building a diversified writing
community" (141).

Matalene's and Mao's responses vis-à-vis the responses of
feminist compositionists to the agonistic nature of Western

persuasive discourse are important to note. Matalene, to be sure, is writing of her experiences as a teacher in China; a pedagogy based upon her experiences would be of limited value in writing classrooms in the United States. Her conclusion suggests only that "our responsibility is surely to try to understand and appreciate [the Chinese tradition], to admit the relativity of our own rhetoric, and to realize that logics different from our own are not necessarily illogical" (806). However, the composition textbooks from which Mao quotes suggest that she is thinking of first-year composition classes when she asks, "What, if anything, can we do with this new model of persuasive discourse in our writing classrooms?" (140). At the very least, she hopes that the classroom practice that she proposes will "foster a much needed sense of diversity" and a "comfortable" feeling for students "regardless of their rhetoric backgrounds" (141). Notably absent from Mao's description of such a writing classroom are calls for narrative and journal writing and small groups critiquing one another's papers.

The keeping of personal journals, so enthusiastically recommended by many of the contributors to Caywood and Overing's collection, may seem alien to many non-Western students. Carolyn Matalene explains why "the favorite self-expressive mode of Western writing teachers" made her students in China uncomfortable (791). All of the great religions of China—Confucianism, Taoism, Buddhism—de-emphasize the importance of the individual and, by extension, de-emphasize the importance of self-expression (791). Thus, Chinese writers seek not to express themselves but to "manipulate" their memory banks of classic phrases, to do things the way they have always been done (794). Matalene acknowledges that it took her a while to understand why fewer and fewer of her students handed in journals as the semester progressed. Only after she realized that Mao Zedung's "being united" meant "don't be different" did she understand her students' rhetorical values, so different from her own. Likewise, Fan Shen reports that he was confused when teachers in America told him to "Just write what *you* think" (460). China's political and literary traditions, as well as its religious tradition, require "a timid, humble, modest" I, while his English composition teachers expected a "confident, assertive, aggressive" I (462).

In addition, several composition scholars report that students from other cultures are uncomfortable writing and sharing personal narratives. Sara Kurtz Allaei and Ulla Maija Connor, for example, find that Middle Eastern students are reluctant to share their writing, especially if it is personal writing, with their peers (24). My experience with students from the Middle East is similar. I remember, in particular, one young woman who had been ordered to the writing center to get help on a narrative essay. The student was fluent in seven languages and wrote in a style that was quaintly (but charmingly) old-fashioned, the mark of a student who has been schooled in English elsewhere. Clearly, her writing skills were not the problem here. After some conversation, the real "problem" emerged. With an air of finality, she declared that her personal experiences were none of her teacher's business. Mike Rose reports a similar reluctance among "certain minority cultures" in "Remedial Writing Courses: A Critique and a Proposal" (108). Furthermore, his experience correlates with that of Dolores K. Schriner and Matthew Willen, who found that they had to adapt Bartholomae and Petrosky's *Facts, Artifacts, and Counterfacts* because its "intensive focus on the individual experience during the passage from adolescence to adulthood" was "distant" and "uncomfortable" for "many of their students (especially Native American and Mexican American students) who come from cultures where the ideals of the community supersede those of the individual" (232).

Finally, Robert B. Kaplan questions the value of feminist/ process pedagogy for non-native speakers of English. He states that non-native speakers of English often have a different opinion of what counts as evidence, of the "optimal order" in which to present evidence, and of "the number of evidentiary instances that need to be presented in order to induce conviction in a reader" (10). As a result, non-native speakers of English are not well-served by feminist/process approaches. The emphasis of feminist/process pedagogy on narrative prose and journal keeping does not help students learn to write expository prose. Moreover, he insists that those teaching English as a Second Language must include the "formal teaching" of genre conventions in their classrooms, because such conventions are "probably totally inaccessible to members of other cultures (with different conventions)" (14, 15). Finally, Kaplan contends that despite the similarities between nonnative speakers and "quasi-literate" native speakers, the two groups must be afforded different pedagogies, for to treat both groups alike is to "trivialize" the real differences between them (15). At this point, compositionists might hope that Kaplan would delineate the similarities and differences between these two groups' approaches to writing academic discourse. That he does not is evidence both of contrastive rhetoric's cognitive bent and of what Valdés calls the compartmentalization of composition studies.

Sara Kurtz Allaei and Ulla Maija Connor's perspective on multicultural classrooms draws upon sociolinguistic research on oral interaction and the applied linguistic research area of contrastive rhetoric and concurs in many ways with Kaplan's. Whereas Caywood and Overing see the "creative potential of heterogeneity" (xi), Allaei and Connor demonstrate the difficulties peer collaborative groups pose in multicultural classrooms. Chief among the problems they perceive are these:

> [D]iffering communication styles may lead to conflict among "collaborative" group members and differing notions about conventions of "good" writing may lead to quite different responses to writing from responses a [native-English-speaking] reader might provide. (20)

As a point of interest, Kaplan goes one step further than do Allaei and Connor, noting that some readers "may refuse to interact with a text" at all "as a result of its foreignness" (15). Allaei and Connor's study is particularly informed by Ron Scollon and Suzanne B. K. Scollon's research on Athabaskan-English interethnic communication. Bearing in mind Joan Swann's caution that "any interpretation of conversational features must actually be highly context-specific" (Coates and Cameron 67), Allaei and Connor make it a point to mention that the research of Scollon and Scollon was conducted in educational settings. It is for us to determine how like Athabaskan Indians (of Alaska and Northern Canada) our students of different cultures are. At any rate, the research is interesting, especially in Scollon and Scollon's depiction of Americans as "the extreme case" when speaking of "English speakers" (17).

As Allaei and Connor note, the Scollons' studies confirmed significant cross-cultural differences in the style and patterns of oral interaction between the Athabaskans and American English speakers, differences which impeded conversation and led to frequent miscommunications (20). They found, for instance, that Athabaskans spoke less than American English speakers. Scollon and Scollon claimed that this difference in the amount of talk can be explained by the Athabaskans' perception of conversation as a threat to one's carefully protected individuality and by the American English speakers' reliance on conversation as a way to get to know another person. Not surprisingly, the two groups frequently misunderstood one another: Athabaskans judged American English speakers as overly talkative, while American English speakers thought that the Athabaskans were not interested in a conversation (20–21). Moreover, the Scollons reported that the two groups have exactly opposite expectations of the roles of speaker and listener in conversation. Athabaskans, for example, expect the person in the superordinate position to be the exhibitionist and the person in the subordinate position to be the spectator. American English speakers, however, acting from exactly opposite expectations, expect students to "show off," to talk. Predictably, the two groups miscommunicated; Athabaskans perceived the American English speakers as "egotistical," while American English speakers thought the Athabaskans were "unsure, aimless, withdrawn, or incompetent" (21). (Rosalinda Barrera reports that interactional patterns of American classrooms are contrary to the listen-and-learn home norms of Hispanic students as well [qtd. in Allen 1].)

Using a modified version of Penelope Brown and Stephen C. Levinson's model of the "universal politeness phenomenon," Scollon and Scollon were able to explain the mis-communication between the two groups in terms of differing politeness strategies. The Scollons explained that the Athabaskans used more "deference politeness strategies" ("apologizing, using ambiguous impositions, not stating impositions at all") in order to secure a "hearer's right to independence and autonomy." Conversely, American English speakers used more "solidarity politeness strategies" ("clear direct statements in which the speaker claims to be part of the same group as the hearer, assuming reciprocity") in order to attend to a "hearer's wants and needs" (21). K. H. Basso's study of Western Apache culture reports findings similar to the Scollons'. When strangers meet in the Western Apache culture, Basso explains, no one feels compelled to introduce one to another. In fact, if a stranger is quick to launch into conversation, he or she will be regarded with "undisguised suspicion." Moreover, if the stranger is an "Anglo," it is usually assumed that "he wants to teach us something" or that "he wants to make friends in a hurry." Basso further explains that Western Apaches are "extremely reluctant" to make friends in a hurry, for they regard the establishment of social relations as a "serious matter that calls for caution, careful judgment, and plenty of time" (173).

All in all, Allaei and Connor conclude that "conflict, or at the least, very high levels of discomfort, may occur in multicultural collaborative peer response groups" (22). The "we're-in-this-together-so-let's-talk-about-our-writing" strategy that is so much a part of the structure of collaborative groups, Allaei and Connor contend, is based on a solidarity model of politeness, a model that the Scollons have cautioned against using in multicultural classrooms. Ashton-Jones has already suggested that feminist compositionists "check *some* of their unfettered enthusiasm for collaborative pedagogies" (31). Both Basso's and Allaei and Connor's observations suggest that teachers of multicultural groups do likewise. As Allaei and Connor argue, students from other cultures may be unfamiliar with, and therefore uncomfortable with, the communicative style of collaborative groups. Furthermore, their conclusion underscores the wisdom of Mao's omission (intended or not) of peer groups from her pedagogy designed to foster a "comfortable" feeling in students with different backgrounds in rhetoric.

Allaei and Connor's study is informed by studies in contrastive rhetoric as well as by those in sociolinguistics. Implications from studies in contrastive rhetoric are particularly important for multicultural writing classes, for these have shown that different cultures often define "appropriate" topics for writing differently and esteem different communication styles, differences that impact these classes (24). Using evidence from informal surveys that they have conducted in their own multicultural classes of non-native English-speaking students, Allaei and Connor uncover three areas of concern. First, East Asian students, in particular, say that they are uncomfortable making negative comments on other students' drafts. Allaei and Connor attribute this phenomenon to these students' reliance on deference politeness strategies. Second, they find that Middle Eastern students do not like to share their writing with their peers. Finally, they report that varying levels of English proficiency complicated peer collaborative activities (24). Concluding their study with several practical suggestions that could help peer response groups succeed in multicultural classrooms, they acknowledge that their focus has been limited to peer response groups in multicultural classes of non-native English-speaking students. Allaei and Connor nonetheless suggest that their workshopping and peer reviewing activities will be "highly beneficial" for classes comprised of both native and non-native speakers (27).

Messages sent by both feminist compositionists and instructors of non-native English speakers concern me. Compartmentalized as both groups are in the field of composition, feminist compositionists and English as a Second Language instructors alike offer broad applications of pedagogical approaches based upon limited, context-specific experiences. Sociolinguists caution again and again that research on conversational style is highly context-specific (see, for example, Cameron, McAlinden, and O'Leary; Swann; Coates and Cameron). However, as their scholarship is appropriated by other fields, that message gets lost. Like Valdés, Barrie Thorne, Cheris Kramarae, and Nancy Henley point out that "there has been remarkably little research on the intersection of gender, race, social class, and sexualities," and assert the need for "more extensive theoretical and empirical research" in these areas (20).

Deborah Tannen's recent analysis of conversation in a graduate class attempts a brief look at the interaction of gender and culture. Enrolled in Tannen's class were twenty students, eleven women and nine men. She found that six of the men spoke at least occasionally in class; the three who did not were Asian (two Japanese and one Chinese); the only other foreign male student, a Syrian, did contribute. Five of the women did not speak at all, but only one was foreign (Japanese) ("Teachers" B3). Noting that several of the students were not comfortable speaking to the whole group, Tannen placed them in small groups six times during the semester. She used three different "constellations": by degree program, by gender, and by conversational style (for example, fast talkers together, quiet talkers together, and Asian students together). Directing the students to look upon the groups "as examples of interactional data and to note the different ways they participated" (B3), Tannen discovered that the students "overwhelmingly" preferred it when she grouped them by gender. Foreign students preferred being grouped together as well ("Analyzing" 8). Tannen herself observed that women who had never spoken in class were busily conversing in the small groups. Curiously, the Japanese woman mentioned that she found it difficult to contribute to the all-woman group because the other women were so talkative. Tannen finds this observation particularly revealing, for it shows that the "same person who can be 'oppressed' into silence in one context can become the talkative 'oppressor' in another" ("Teachers" B3). All in all, Tannen argues that Americans as a "source of pride" ignore issues of gender and ethnicity (the "I treat everyone the same" syndrome [B3] reminiscent of Thomas Fox's Mr. H discussed in Chapter 2 of this study).

Nevertheless, she maintains that "treating people the same is not equal treatment if they are not the same"

("Teachers" B3). In the end, Tannen recommends "segregation," at least some of the time, into same-gender and same-culture groups, for these groups give students a "chance to be more comfortable," thus bringing out their abilities ("Analyzing" 8). Although Tannen calls for teachers "to be aware of differences of gender and culture among students" (8), respondents to Tannen's piece in the *Chronicle* contend that her awareness is stereotypical and reductive. Donald Ellis, a professor of communication at the University of Hartford, complains that "Tannen drags out the old stereotypes, that women are oriented toward cooperation and relationships while men are adversarial and hierarchical, then uses these as explanations of different patterns of participation" (B2). Patricia Laurence points out that there are many kinds of silences exhibited by women and minorities and that we must "resist classifying present styles of keeping silence, reflecting or learning in essentialist terms" (B2). Although I question whether many compositionists would find the results of Tannen's informal study as "shocking" as she suspects ("Analyzing" 8), her study does point up the need for scholarship investigating the intersection of gender, race, and class both in classroom interactions and in student negotiations of the conventions of academic discourse.

MAKING ROOM FOR MANY VOICES

Compositionists must realize, as Valdés suggests, that our field is one of compartmentalization, that we who are by now well-schooled in the difficulties that many women experience with academic discourse are probably not well-schooled in the difficulties students from other cultures experience when faced with tasks the academy equates with academic literacy. We must also realize that in order to work effectively, we need to have extensive knowledge about this new population, a knowledge not currently available.

One step to improve this situation has just been taken by the Conference on College Composition and Communication. "Scholars for the Dream," a new program instituted both to encourage scholarship by African Americans, Asian Americans, Native Americans, and Hispanic/Latino Americans and to further their involvement in the profession, will award up to ten scholarships for first-time presenters at its annual conventions, beginning in 1993. However, I agree with Valdés's contention that such actions must not be regarded as more than a first step. What she feels is essential is the commitment of "mainstream" compositionists to make bilingual minority students a professionwide concern, not just the priority of a few specialists whose names are probably unknown to most readers of *College Composition and Communication* or even *English in the Two-Year College* (113). On another level, Edelsky, Valdés, and John Ogbu all recommend ethnographic studies of the home cultures of minority students—Hopi, Chinese, Chicano, and so on—in order to determine the social status, age, gender, and societal status of those who write in the first language and for what purposes. Ogbu claims that careful ethnographic research can identify cultural differences that can cause problems for minority and non-Western students in Western classrooms and can propose specific programs to reduce cultural dissonance for these students in Western classrooms (45–46).

But these solutions are years away. In the meantime, "we must try not to do harm" (Holzman 138). We must guard against making our classrooms chilly places for students unfamiliar with and uncomfortable with Western discourse conventions. I am not suggesting that we should abandon collaborative peer groups, but we may want to think about how we can configure them. Sometimes we may want to "segregate" our students by culture or gender. More importantly, we must share our stories and the stories of our students with others, at conferences, in articles, in conversations. Most importantly, we must become students of our students' literacies, for in learning from one another and from our students, we may avoid harm.

5

Reading-to-Write/Writing-to-Read; Conversations in the Academy

> Maybe we need, as writers, teachers, readers
> who would talk to students—all students—
> novelization of the languages we use. In
> novelized languages, no one speaks with a
> single voice because any utterance contains
> within it traces of past conversations; in
> novelized languages, all claims and all
> propositions contain within them their own
> adversatives, their own contradictions, their
> contingent modifiers. It is that kind of language
> that may open itself to possibilities for
> convergence in its openness to past and future
> human concerns, those that concern us all.
> —Jay L. Robinson

In the preceding chapters, I have examined class, gender, and culture as factors that marginalize students and their teachers in relation to language use and language instruction. In these discussions, I have sought to demonstrate that studies in the field of composition isolate class or gender or culture as marginalizing factors and have suggested that one direction for future research is the investigation of the interaction of these factors. Furthermore, I have argued that radical pedagogies (whether perceived as feminist or Freirean), in their attempts to add previously disenfranchised voices to the discourse of the academy, have likewise focused on class or gender or culture, thereby overlooking (or perhaps, merely downplaying) how complex the problem of silence and the solution to it is in the academy. As I have shown, an uncritical adoption of feminist pedagogies—narrative writing, journal keeping, for instance—may silence students from non-Western cultures, while adoption of the same pedagogy for both quasi-literate English speakers and non-native English speakers ignores the real differences between these groups of students. I have attributed much of this too-narrow focus in composition studies both to compartmentalization within the field itself (as demonstrated by a comparison of membership rolls of Teachers of English to Speakers of Other Languages and the National Council of Teachers of English) and to absence in the professional journals of those voices who teach most of the writing courses in postsecondary institutions in the United States.

In this chapter, I turn to the intersection of disciplines rather than to the isolation of them in the field of composition studies. I demonstrate that despite the pervasiveness of reading-to-write pedagogies in the fields of basic writing, feminist composition, and English as a Second Language instruction, few studies focus on the relationship of reading to writing. In addition, I consider the centrality of the "conversation" metaphor in discussions of reading and writing, suggesting that reading-as-conversation, like social conversations themselves, is a more complex construct than some compositionists have realized. Finally, I provide a "snapshot" of Ms. L, a returning, part-time student in her mid-forties, showing how her personal background helped to shape her response to a research paper assignment and how my interviews with her helped me to understand better how her reading informed her writing.

READING-TO-WRITE PEDAGOGIES

However compartmentalized basic writing education, feminist composition, or English as a Second Language instruction may be in the field, theorist/practitioners of each of these "specialties" advance pedagogies that incorporate reading as well as writing. Charles Bazerman notes that this increasing interest in the pedagogy of writing about reading began in the late 1970s (Rev. 241). Perhaps the best known example from basic writing pedagogy is David Bartholomae and Anthony Petrosky's *Facts, Artifacts and Counterfacts.* Bartholomae and Petrosky explain that their goal is "to develop, through dialogue, an enabling language," one that can give students who have been identified as poor readers and writers a way to transform "the ways they see, and thereby, participate in the world" (15, 30). Their first-year composition course pairs a sequence of writing assignments with a corresponding sequence of reading assignments. The coauthors further explain that they try to choose writing assignments that reflect "powerful and pressing" themes rooted in their students' experiences. Their writing classes focus on revision and editing, and their reading assignments move from first-person and fictional accounts to works by authorities in the fields of anthropology, sociology, and so on (30). Although Bartholomae and Petrosky's six-credit course is among the most intensive of basic writing courses, its integration of reading and writing is no longer unusual. Glynda Hull and Mike Rose note that "one of the interesting things" that they have observed during the several years that they have been conducting research on remedial writing instruction in American colleges and universities is "the integration of reading, and particularly the reading about literature, into the remedial writing classroom" (" 'This' " 287).

Bartholomae and Petrosky's course is used for students marginalized by culture as well as by class. The English department at Northern Arizona University, for example, selected and adapted the course in an attempt to stem the disproportionately high attrition rates of students of Native American and Mexican American descent. The department's development of a new composition program, underwritten by a three-year Ford Foundation grant, was intended to provide for "more effective literacy instruction and lead to greater equity in educational opportunities among students from all racial and ethnic groups" (Schriner and Willen 230). Because the Arizona Board of Regents will not permit universities to offer remedial courses, the *Facts* course at Northern Arizona cannot properly be labeled a "basic" writing course. However, university data show that students from ethnic and minority groups report difficulty with conventions of academic discourse—a phenomenon typical of many basic writers—as a "primary factor" in their dropping out (Schriner and Willen 231).

Victor Villanueva explains how the syllabus for the new first-year composition course, by incorporating a dialectical relationship between tradition and change, attempts to balance the Regents' mandates with the needs of racially and ethnically diverse students. Reading assignments juxtapose works with a traditional worldview from the American traditional canon—Hemingway or Steinbeck, for instance—with non-traditional works with different worldviews from outside the canon—Caroline Maria deJesus's *Child of the Dark* or Buchi Emecheta's *Double Yoke*, for example. To tie the readings to what Bartholomae and Petrosky call the "powerful and pressing" themes rooted in students' experiences, Villanueva's writing assignments follow a "set series about conflicts [students] have had to confront" and ask students to "consider the sources of these conflicts" (259). By incorporating a dialectical relationship between tradition and change, the course attempts to foster critical consciousness in both traditional students and those from ethnically and racially diverse backgrounds. All in all, Villanueva hopes that this dialectic will not only provide a way for students to "acquire the literate, academic culture" but will make them more critically conscious of "their often antagonistic relationship to it" (260).

Just as there is a wide acceptance of the integration of reading and writing in first-year composition courses designed to empower writers marginalized by class or race or ethnicity, so, too, is there a wide acceptance of the integration of reading and writing in feminist composition pedagogy. Elizabeth A. Flynn, for one, integrates reading and writing in composition courses where issues of gender have center stage. In a recent review of *The Gender Reader*, a collection of essays focusing on the question of gender, Flynn calls for other editors to assemble similar collections suitable for students taking composition courses or women's studies courses in the hopes that the "availability of such books" will help "rectify social and political inequities" (225). Another reviewer reiterates Flynn's hope and recommends the collection for use in courses on gender issues. Pointing out the editors' emphasis on dialogue among students, Doris M. Piatek envisions these discussions about the collected essays as "a way to play a role in shaping society for the future" (70).

In addition, all but one of the four essays addressing issues of "Equity in Practice" in Cynthia L. Caywood and Gillian R. Overing's *Teaching Writing* collection integrate reading and writing. Donna Perry assigns readings from women's journals in her required introductory-level women's writing course so that her students will have an opportunity to write about such "taboo" subjects as homosexuality and abortion in their own journals (152). James D. Riemer combines readings of essays on gender roles with essay and journal writing in his honors composition class in order to "prompt students to question society's rigidly defined gender roles" and "to become aware of the ways in which these roles affect their own lives." He selects essays that will challenge his students' traditional, conservative views of sex roles and encourage them to give thoughtful consideration to "feminist, liberal" views of gender roles (157). Finally, Mickey Pearlman describes the integration of reading and writing in her writing course which focuses on questions of equity and feminism. The first assignment in the course, for instance, requires students to read Judy Syfer's "I Want a Wife" before they write on the topic, "How I Would Liberate My Mother," or "How I Would Liberate My Father in Order to Liberate My Mother."

Two common threads tie these oft-times compartmentalized divisions of composition studies together: the integration of reading and writing and the centrality of the metaphor of dialogue or conversation. I will examine the implications of the conversation metaphor after a brief discussion of the small number of studies on the interaction of reading and writing, what Linda Flower terms "reading-to-write." Clearly, as Hull and Rose have illustrated, reading, and especially reading about literature, has become a staple of writing courses designed to improve critical consciousness in students marginalized by class, gender, or culture (" 'This' " 287). Moreover, Flower maintains that reading-to-write is the "task" most often asked of students in all college-level work, but one that has been ignored in most writing research to date (4, 6). Even fewer studies focus on the underprepared student, Hull and Rose assert ("Rethinking" 142). Their finding is especially significant in the light of current trends in enrollment in postsecondary institutions of learning. For example, because of a combination of declining birth rates and an expanding system of higher education, if every student who graduated from a U.S. high school were to go to college and stayed there for four years, there would still be room for more students at four-year institutions and no students left over for two-year institutions (Finn 114). As a result, institutions of higher education will fill their empty places with a larger percentage of both traditional college-age and older students; many of these students will be labeled "underprepared."

The few studies that do consider underprepared students' writing are, for the most part, text-based analyses, studies like Mina Shaughnessy's *Errors and Expectations*. However valuable these studies may be, they cannot account for the socio-cognitive factors that contribute to the production of underprepared students' texts, Hull and Rose point out ("Rethinking" 142). The few available studies on college-age students' reading skills describe the difficulties that poor college-age readers have in determining main ideas, drawing inferences, and evaluating their understanding of the text, but, like research on writing, these studies provide few clues as to what happens when students are required to read in order to write (Hull and Rose, "Rethinking" 143).

READING AND WRITING AS CONVERSATION

"A Relationship between Reading and Writing: The Conversational Model," "Collaborative Learning and the

'Conversation of Mankind,'" "Peer Tutoring and the 'Conversation of Mankind,'" *Conversations on the Written Word*—the metaphor of literacy activities as conversation is central to the field of composition studies. No doubt Kenneth Burke's analogy of history and the history of ideas as an unending conversation is one source of this metaphor. Burke uses an extended analogy of a cocktail party to explain his concept of history:

> Imagine that you enter a parlor. You come late. When you arrive, others have long preceded you, and they are engaged in a heated discussion, a discussion too heated for them to pause and to tell you exactly what it is all about. In fact, the discussion had already begun long before any of them got there, so that no one present is qualified to retrace for you all of the steps that have gone on before. You listen for a moment, until you decide that you have caught the tenor of the argument; then you put in your oar. Someone answers; you answer him: another comes to your defense; another aligns himself against you, to either the embarrassment or gratification of your opponent, dependent upon the quality of your ally's assistance. However, the discussion is interminable. The hour grows late, you must depart. And you do depart, with the discussion still vigorously in progress. (110–11)

Burke's analogy suggests that a newcomer can enter an ongoing conversation as soon as he or she has caught on to what is being talked about. What is not considered in his analogy, or in Bazerman's, Kenneth Bruffee's, or Jay Robinson's, is the miscommunication that many sociolinguists describe as taking place in cross-cultural conversations.

The conversational model that Bazerman proposes in "A Relationship between Reading and Writing" presumes that students, if properly instructed, will have a fairly easy entry into literate conversations. To be sure, Bazerman's principal intent is to point out the limitations of expressivist approaches to writing instruction with their emphasis on the individual writer at the expense of a consideration of the contexts in which writing takes place. The conversational model that he offers as a "remedy" acknowledges that different conversations are "familiar and important to students," but does not consider what happens when conversations are familiar to some students but alien to others (658). In Bazerman's scheme, once students acquire an accurate understanding of prior comments and are able to react to and evaluate readings, they can then define issues that they wish to pursue, and, like Burke's party goer putting in an oar, they will easily be drawn into "wider public, professional, and academic communities" (661).

For Bruffee and Robinson, writing and conversation are rather seamlessly joined. Bruffee defines writing as "temporarily and functionally related to conversation"; in fact, it is "a technologically displaced form of conversation." Bruffee's model writing classrooms are collaborative so that students have an opportunity to engage in conversation—peer collaboration—during all phases of the writing process ("Peer" 7). Especially important to note is the role Bruffee assigns to collaborative learning: "It provides a particular kind of social context for conversation . . . that of status equals, or peers" (8).

Throughout *Conversations on the Written Word*, Robinson employs the conversation metaphor just as unproblematically. He speaks of composition courses "deliberately designed to treat talk and writing as seamless uses of language" (164). Only in the Afterword does Robinson acknowledge that times have so changed since he penned many of the essays in this collection that the metaphor of literacy as conversation is no longer appropriate. Robinson recognizes, as Bruffee and Bazerman do not, that languages are exclusive, and that they exclude not only those who do not use their specialized vocabularies, but especially those whose gender, race, class, or ethnicity have placed them on the margins before a conversation even begins. He suggests another metaphor, borrowed from Mikhail Bakhtin, of "novelized languages," the explanation of which provides the epigraph for this chapter. Cheryl Geisler joins Robinson in questioning the utility of the metaphor of literacy as conversation. Her study of the reading and writing strategies of "disciplinary insiders" and "novices" has led her to conclude that "a purely conversational model of literacy may be missing the point of why individuals propose and maintain written interaction in the first place": to create special abstract mental models (172, 184).

Studies from sociolinguistics would suggest that conversations are more problematic than those who use the literacy-as-conversation metaphor allow. For example, sociolinguist Deborah Tannen, who sees life itself as a "series of conversations," shows how conversational differences between men and women often lead them to interpret the same conversation differently (*You* 13). If reading and writing are perceived as "conversations" with a written text, might not these differences in conversational style apply to the acts of reading and writing as well? Chapter 3 describes several studies that demonstrate that women's approaches to writing are different from those of men (see Flynn, "Composing," and Cayton, "What," for example).

Recently, studies from cognitive science and reader-response criticism have shown that men and women read differently, too. Mary Crawford and Roger Chaffin state that experiments conducted by cognitive scientists provide limited evidence that men and women do not interpret words in texts in the same way and that "gender or gender role identification should play a large part in determining how texts are understood" (4). David Bleich's and Flynn's studies of college-age readers show differences in men's and women's responses to narrative texts (Bleich, *Double*; Flynn, "Gender"). In reading "conversations," Bleich finds that women are more inclined than men to enter into the human relationships in the stories, to identify with several of the characters, and "to experience the reading as a variety of emotions" (153). Men, on the other hand, are more detached, more likely to judge the individual characters, and more likely to identify with just one or two characters (154). Like Bleich's, Flynn's study reveals that women participate in the events of the stories while men remain detached. Furthermore, she cautiously concludes that women's characteristic patterns of speech are "transformed into useful interpretive strategies— receptivity and yet critical assessment of the text—in the act of reading" (266).

Hull and Rose's current research project is concerned with literacy conversations in remedial classrooms, so often populated with students marginalized by class and culture. They argue that given this "rich mix of class and culture," as reading becomes an integral part of these classrooms, "composition teachers will increasingly be called on to explore questions of interpretation, expectation, and background knowledge" (" 'This' " 287). Hull and Rose themselves use the "conversation" metaphor, but unlike Bazerman and Bruffee, they acknowledge that differences in conversational style may impede knowledge-making in the classroom. In particular, they have found that a "conversational pattern" in remedial reading and writing classes that channels students from non-mainstream cultures into "more 'efficient' discourse," may also "socialize students into a mode of interaction that will limit rather than enhance their participation in intellectual work" (296). A case study from this most current research project (focusing on the "most remedial" writing and reading classes in community colleges, state colleges, and universities) shows how one student's (Maria's) conversational style—whether influenced by previous school experiences or shaped by family dynamics—did not abide by the tacit rules governing turn-taking in the class. As a result, her teacher labeled her "Queen of the Non Sequiturs" and shut her out of knowledge-making activities in the classroom (Hull et al 304, 311).

I am particularly drawn to Hull and Rose's research project. They aim to provide a series of "snapshots" of underprepared students, thick descriptions of the "knowledge, assumptions, and behaviors that characterize and influence underprepared students' creation and use of texts." Ultimately, they hope that their case studies will provide "epiphanies" that "will move us all toward a different and richer representation of literacy instruction for underprepared students" ("Rethinking" 153). Three of their recent articles have provided pictures of Maria (Hull et al), a student in a remedial classroom at an urban college; Robert, a student in the most remedial composition class at the University of California, Los Angeles (" 'This' "); and Tanya, a student in a basic reading and writing class (much like an adult literacy class) in an urban community college ("Rethinking"). For the remainder of this chapter, I am going to offer another case, one inspired by their studies.

The Case of "Ms. L"

The snapshot that I offer of Ms. L., however, differs from those of Hull and Rose in its focus and choice of lens. Hull and Rose's research centers on students in the most remedial classes in the institutions that they visit. The multifaceted lens that they train on their data (texts, videotapes of classroom interaction, audiotapes of tutorial sessions, speak-aloud and stimulated-recall sessions) attempts to integrate social-cultural and cognitive approaches to "problematic reading and writing" ("Rethinking" 152). My study, on the other hand, seeks to extend Hull and Rose's work in its focus on one of the new faces that *Time* magazine predicts will populate college campuses by the year 2000: part-time, older students taking courses to change careers (Elson 54, 55). Moreover, my snapshot uses a phenomenological lens, one of the "new methods" that Flynn says are needed for new research questions that such studies as Hull and Rose's pose ("Composing 'Composing' " 84), and an approach to which mainstream journals now seem more open (Gebhardt 9). In Flynn's words, my study is situated "on the blurred edges of several traditions, for it is clearly not an experiment nor an ethnography nor even so detailed a case study as are Hull and Rose's. Like Flynn, I am interpreting a student's text through the lens of Belenky and her colleagues' scholarship on women's ways of knowing; and, like Hull and Rose, I am trying to provide another answer to one of their questions: What tends to happen to the productive and unproductive strategies, habits, rules, and assumptions characteristic of underprepared students' writing and reading skills during instruction? ("Rethinking" 152).

By way of an answer, I will examine versions of one

student's term paper and interviews that I conducted with her six months after she had submitted the final version of it. I will note the ways in which the student's personal background shaped her response to the assignment, and the ways the term paper changed. Further, I will show how my initial feminist reading of these changes, based upon text analysis, was inaccurate.

The term paper that I am going to analyze comes from a student who was enrolled in a Composition II course that I taught at a small, suburban campus in an open admissions community college. Many of its students come from a tightly knit Greek community, where Greek, not English, is the first language of even its American-born members. Students are placed in composition classes based upon their performance on the Test of Standard Written English and a holistically scored twenty-minute writing sample. Ms. L's test scores placed her in Composition I, but samples of her prose that I include here—sometimes incoherent, sometimes lacking in development—illustrate that in other settings, she would probably have been identified as a "basic writer." The college catalog describes Composition II as a course that "stresses methods of library research and emphasizes writing of the research paper and the paper of literary interpretation. The reading includes selections from at least two forms of literature" (*St. Petersburg* 158). Those who teach and take the course describe it as a textbook case of cognitive overload. After several semesters experimenting with different configurations, I had decided to admit to both my students and myself that the course was schizophrenic; essentially, I had divided the course into separate units: term papers for the first half of the semester and selections from the required literature text, Edgar V. Roberts and Henry E. Jacobs's *Literature: An Introduction to Reading and Writing,* for the second half.

At the beginning of the semester, twenty-four students were enrolled, fifteen women and nine men, but that number had dwindled to fifteen students by the time term papers were due. Twice as many men as women had dropped out, a fact that, in retrospect, makes me wonder, as did Cayton, if some factor could have made these students so "uneasy with the identity construction required by academic discourse" that they dropped the course rather than contend with it ("What" 334–35). At the time, however, I welcomed the thought of fewer papers to grade.

This class was different from other Composition II courses that I have taught in community colleges. For one thing, although withdrawals from Composition II classes are common, an attrition rate of almost 40 percent is not. (In the other section of Composition II that I taught that semester, only three of twenty-two enrolled students dropped.) For another thing, three of the students were among only four who had qualified for Honors Composition I the spring semester before, and six of the original twenty-four students (including the three honors students) had been in a Composition I course that I had taught that previous semester. Even more interesting for my purposes here was the presence of six returning women students in their forties and fifties, two of whom had qualified for the Honors Composition course. So outspoken were some of these women in classroom discussions that Mr. D, the other honors student (who had no difficulty making his views known), sneaked into an earlier Composition II class of mine whenever he could afford to cut his math class, which was also scheduled at that time. I suspect that he felt oppressed by the women's control of the classroom conversation.

The most vocal student was Ms. M, an honors student in her fifties, whose conversational style was one that Tannen describes as "high involvement" and typical of New York City natives of Jewish background (*You* 201). High-involvement speakers give priority to enthusiastic participation and fill in pauses quickly in order to avoid uncomfortable silences (196). Ms. M could have served as a paradigm. In fact, so quick was she to jump into any classroom discussion that her best friend in both Composition I and II, herself an honors student in her fifties and also from New York, had confided in me that she wished that Ms. M would monitor her contributions, so that she could give other students more opportunities to hold the floor.

I assign "argumentative" term papers of fifteen hundred

to two thousand words in Composition II, and both men and women students struggle with the problem of taking a stand and refuting arguments from the other side. To prepare students for research papers that are expected of them in other courses required by the college, I encourage students to see themselves as "unbiased" researchers and likewise encourage them to adopt an "impersonal" voice in their papers. They are permitted to write across the curriculum, but such controversial topics as pornography, abortion, euthanasia, capital punishment, and drug legalization are off limits. Students begin the assignment by submitting an article that, for them, contains a questionable assertion, the "truth" of which they will investigate for their research project. Before they submit drafts of their final research paper, I have them practice their research skills on a shorter paper, written on the same topic. Here are the directions for the short research paper assignment:

> You are to submit a limited research paper (about 500 words). In the course of the paper you should ask your research question, answer that question in a thesis statement, and use two periodical sources for evidence. One of the sources should oppose the other. In addition, you should use in-text documentation and correct works cited forms.
>
> There are specific writing skills that you need to learn. You need an opening that explains the background or issues related to your research question, and you will want to introduce your sources fully and carefully. Finally, you will want to synthesize your conclusion. Do not leave just two opposing views. You must explain why you prefer one.

Allow me to introduce Ms. L. I was not acquainted with her before she became a student in this Composition II class, but I became particularly interested in her when I noticed an unusual change in voice from the time she responded to this first short research paper assignment and the time she submitted her final paper on "the financial effects of divorce." An engaging smile and an open, friendly manner were her most distinguishing characteristics; professors who did not know her often commented on these. Perhaps Ms. M's enthusiastic contributions silenced Ms. L's participation in class discussions, for during the time that we were working on research papers, she did not often participate in classroom discussions, and she struggled to find a voice in her term paper. A woman in her mid-forties, Ms. L had returned to school when her younger child was eighteen months old, some five months before she filed for divorce from her husband of almost twenty years. She discussed her reasons for the divorce and her return to school in an interview that I recorded some six months after her final research paper was submitted. "I knew I was on the right track to get a divorce at that time," she said, explaining that her husband had refused to go to counseling with her, charging, "the only problem we have is you, because you're crazy." At that point, Ms. L continued, "I said, I need to go and get some training." Her return to school was "the beginning of the end" of their marriage. At the time the class was working on research papers, Ms. L and I had talked about how she had felt about returning to school after more than twenty years. I asked her to recall those feelings during our interview. Ms. L replied:

> I think I was stifled to a point because I really had no knowledge of a lot of things that she [her Composition I teacher] was talking about. I was so centered upon my husband that I never took the time to watch the news or TV, and I really don't like to read the paper. I read novels and fiction and different things, but that was for my own enjoyment. I never really paid attention to what was going on in the world, so it was almost like I'd had a space gap in my life that was totally void of all these things. And it was a shocking discovery when I found out and realized what was going on [in the world].

I knew that Ms. L liked to write poetry, for she had brought in several of the poems that she had written in the early hours of the morning for me to comment upon and had confided that for her birthday, she had asked her father to buy her a ream of "good paper" to print them on. In fact, she had submitted several poems to the college literary magazine and to a poetry contest advertised in a magazine. She even read

Writer's Digest. She wrote short stories, too, and I had lent her some of my literature anthologies so that she could see how experienced writers handled dialogue and pace.

Analysis. I am going to begin explicating Ms. L's work with the essay that she submitted in response to the limited research paper assignment. She had chosen two articles reprinted in a volume of *Opposing Viewpoints,* one written by an associate professor of sociology at Harvard, the other by the manager of education for a computer corporation who had "researched divorce extensively." Although one article was four pages long and the other five, Ms. L highlighted just four sentences in both articles combined. Printed below are the first sentences from the article written by the Harvard professor. I have italicized the only sentence Ms. L had high-lighted in that article:

> Divorce has radically different economic consequences for men and women. While most divorced men find that their standard of living improves after divorce, most divorced women and minor children in their households find that their standard of living plummets. This [viewpoint] *shows that when income is compared to needs, divorced men experience an average 42 percent rise in their standard of living in the first year after the divorce, while divorced women (and their children) experience a 73 percent decline.*

Ms. L uses the italicized sentence in the first paragraphs in both her short and final research papers. The opening paragraphs of her short research paper are printed below (the italicized quotes from Susan Anderson-Khleif represent two of the three passages Ms. L had highlighted in her second source):

> (1) Although fathers feel they are "pinned to the wall" financially after a divorce (Anderson-Khleif 205), women not only have to deal with financial devastation, but assume full responsibility of their children, home, and the fact that they will never bring in the income at a level anywhere near their exspouses. With all things taken into account, who does become more financially devastated, the husband or the wife? (2) Susan Anderson-Khleif points out in an article called

Divorce Devastates Men's Standard of Living that *"the major-ity of men she interviewed were ordered to pay 25 to 50 percent of their net income in child support or alimony to their exwives"* (206). This left them at a very low income rate which when combined with the loss of their home and other personal property, left them at near poverty levels. Meanwhile Lenore J. Weitzman, who wrote *Divorce Devastates Women's Standard of Living, "shows that when income is compared to needs, divorced men experience an average 43 percent* rise *in their standard of living in the first year after divorce, while the divorced woman (and their children) experience a 73 percent* decline*"* (201). (Ms. L's italics)

(3) Divorce alone can be devastating to the family unit, not even taking in to account any financial or property settle-ments. Divorce if spelled out means the following: D- destruction, I-inconsiderate, V- violence, O- obstinacy, R- re-venge, C- catastrophic, and E- ever growing hate. Though these things may not appear all at one time, they seem to pop up periodically during the divorce process and can be mild to a degree of severity that closely resembles insanity [sic].

In the first two paragraphs, Ms. L is clearly attempting to respond to the directions in the assignment: she poses her research question at the end of the first paragraph; she uses the standard "although . . . but" formula to make clear that her choice of topic is argumentative; and she is careful to "introduce" her sources by naming the article that each author has written. (In subsequent paragraphs, Ms. L further identifies Weitzman as "an associate professor of sociology at Harvard University in Cambridge, Mass." and Anderson-Khleif as "a member of education and training for Digital Equipment Corporation's Storage Systems division, [who] has done extensive research on divorce in the U.S. and abroad.")

Although the prose of the first two paragraphs lacks the polish of a more experienced writer, Ms. L's attempt to appropriate the distinctive register of academic discourse— her use of the "although" clause, her avoidance of plagiarism by changing "near-poverty level incomes" in the source to "very low income rate" in her own paper—would most likely have been acceptable, if not well-rewarded, in other courses.

But her third paragraph displayed just the sort of emotional involvement in an "objective" term paper that was certain to make life difficult for Ms. L in her other courses. In my subsequent interviews with her, she told me that she had made up the "D-I-V-O-R-C-E" example herself. Nor was that paragraph the only one to depend more upon emotional than logical appeal. In her next paragraph, Ms. L describes the "devastating" effects of divorce on men:

> The man may have other added obligations, insurance, dental bills, and so on, which once paid leaves him with barely enough monies to survive on (206). [Anderson-Khleif] claims most fathers must work two jobs then sit back and watch as their support money goes to boyfriends, and his liberated wife's education (207). She also claims that the exhausted husband is given "hassles" on visitation and verbally put down in front of his children (207). When a father does get visitation, he must come up with the money to be able to do something with his children. Thusly the father is totally "cleaned out" (208).

The emotional tone of Ms. L's paper is, in part, a reflection of the tone of the sources that she used. The editors of *Opposing Viewpoints*, for example, had chosen to title the excerpt from Weitzman's *The Divorce Revolution* as "Divorce Devastates Women's Standard of Living." Likewise they chose "Divorce Devastates Men's Standard of Living" for the excerpt from Anderson-Khleif's *Divorced But Not Disastrous*. Furthermore, most of the evidence Anderson-Khleif presents for her position comes from interviews that she had conducted with divorced fathers. The carefully documented examples that Ms. L offers to support the "devastating" financial effects of divorce on men come from these interviews. The tone of the following example is typical of the ten interviews Anderson-Khleif includes, and Ms. L uses the italicized phrase in the opening sentence of her paper:

> I was told if I ever fell short of the $75.00 she'd take me to court. With these new laws, I'd like to see females paying alimony! Women's Lib, but when it comes to the courts, the poor little defenseless thing. Even though she's making $16,000. The guy's getting *pinned to the wall*. These are the

hassles I did not want. I walked away with my clothes. I may just do it sometime [fall short of the support payment] to see if she really would [take me to court]. (working class father, daughters 4 and 6)

But the emotional tone of Anderson-Khleif's interviews only partly explains the emotional tone of Ms. L's paper. When Anderson-Khleif describes "Fathers Grants for Children," a program designed to supplant the welfare programs many women and children depend upon after divorce, she no longer relies on interviews, and her tone is less emotional:

Fathers Grants for Children could be designed as time-limited support (cash transfers) that would be available to separated and divorced fathers who are otherwise unable to pay regular child support during the period of peak economic distress following separation and divorce.

Ms. L reflects this change in tone as well when she says, " 'Fathers Grants for Children is a group which gives grants to fathers that need the support money during the first years of divorce. As their income increases, the grants would decrease until the father was again financially stable' (209)."

It is in Ms. L's selection of evidence from Weitzman's piece that I find a clue to unproductive reading strategies that underprepared reeders employ when reading-to-write. This paragraph illustrates how Ms. L chooses evidence:

[Weitzman] shows though studies done by the U.S. Department of Labor how a woman's standard of living drops 73 percent during the first year while a man's rises 42 percent (202). What does this statistic mean? "It means living on the edge or living without" (202). Food intake is greatly reduced, cars may be sold to get monies needed to buy items for the children, clothing is received through charity or purchased at second hand shops. The children can't stay in their normal activities because of lack of funds. How can this be? "The explanation lies first in the inadequacy of the court's awards, second in the expanded demands on the wife's resources after divorce, and third in the husband's greater earning capacity and ability to supplement his income." (203)

Evidence in Weitzman's article itself comes from studies of families in Michigan and California, a sociologist, and the National Advisory Council on Economic Opportunity. Instead of highlighting the evidence from two full pages of sociological and economic explanations (replete with such terms as "feminization of poverty," "absolute dollars," "differential disadvantage of women's employment") that Weitzman includes to support her conclusion that "men experience a 42 percent improvement in their postdivorce standard of living, while women experience a 73 percent decline," Ms. L chooses to cite the examples that Weitzman offers following the statement, "It is difficult to absorb the full implications of these statistics. What does it mean to have a 73 percent decline in one's standard of living?" The examples that follow recount stories of "macaroni and cheese five nights a week," sewing together "two old dresses to make one outfit," "splurging at the Salvation Army—the only 'new clothes' [the children] got that year." These examples become tales of reduced food intake and secondhand clothing purchases in Ms. L's paraphrase.

Ms. L, like the students in the studies cited by Hull and Rose, had difficulty knowing what was important and focused on details—examples that Weitzman presents— rather than on the implications of the study ("Rethinking" 143). Her self-described reading habits (fiction and novels rather than the newspaper) had left her underprepared for the research paper assignment, for they would have given her little experience analyzing arguments. Moreover, like Hull and Rose's "Tanya," the examples that Ms. L selects to include in the paper are chosen not because they were important to the original text, but because they are important to her ("Rethinking" 149). In a sense, she becomes so wrapped up in the examples that parallel her own experiences that she "dominates" the text, in Flynn's terms; her "memory dominates over experience" and she does not move very far beyond herself ("Gender" 268, 269). The conclusion of Ms. L's short research paper expresses the anger that she felt for her husband at this time:

With both points of view addressed and having gone through a divorce myself; my sympathy lies with the exwife and the children. Due to devoting their life to their husbands and families, once a woman gets divorced her standard of living does drop greatly. She not only has the burden of being a full-time single parent, the upkeep of the home (if she's lucky to get it or at least keep it until the youngest child is 18); she must try to reenter a work field where she has been absent from for a long time. Even with alimony and child support set at the guide lines, keeping the family above the poverty level is extremely difficult. In turn the man walks away to start a new life; financially he will help and in rare cases he will assume some parenting responsibilities, but the norm is to slowly get on with their new lives and leave their old ones behind. This includes visits with children and keeping up his financial aid.

New laws need to be made and followed through; hopefully one day the woman and children of divorce will not come out being so completely devastated. The thought of the effects of this devastation on the children is scary, what will their adulthood and relationships be like?

Once again, Ms. L's conclusion illustrates that she was trying to complete the assignment successfully, for the final directions tell her to explain why she preferred one view, and she clearly makes her position known. What would I do? Ms. L had tried so hard to complete an unfamiliar assignment but had produced a paper that few in the academy would judge as acceptable. Well-steeped as I was that semester in theories of women's ways of writing (I had presented a paper on *Women's Ways of Knowing* at a college-wide in-service just three days before term papers were due), I was especially torn between the possibility that I might be silencing my students' voices by insisting upon an argumentative term paper and the realization that this was the last required writing course, the last chance most students would have to learn the conventions of academic discourse. I was not surprised that Ms. L had interwoven her personal experience into her argument, for women's writing is often characterized as personal and connected. I also knew that although I might be open to alternate approaches to a research paper, professors in her other classes were not. I recommended to Ms. L that she might want to try a more objective approach, one that might concentrate on the financial effects of divorce on the wife, husband, and children.

Just a few weeks later, Ms. L submitted her final research paper with this new beginning:

> The ease in which to obtain a divorce today is mind boggling; it is almost easier to get a divorce than to remain married. Thus the divorce has become all to common place in today's society. Everyone concerned in a divorce is touched by it in one way or another, but the question of who is really financially affected most by a divorce is a major controversy. There have been many books and articles printed in attempt to settle the argument as to who is most affected financially after a divorce. After much study and reading I've come to see that the woman is really the person who ends up being financially affected the most. Dr. Lenore J. Weitzman, an associate professor of sociology at Harvard University in Cambridge, Massachusetts wrote *Divorce Devastates Woman's Standard of Living*. She presents through studies done by the U.S. Department of Labor, how a woman's standard of living drops 73 percent during the first year, while a man's standard of living rises 42 percent during the same time (202).

Ms. L sounds confident in this version. Her extensive reading of "many books and articles" lends authority to her voice. "With information from both sides we will attempt to ascertain who is really affected the most financially after a divorce," she says a few lines later. In this final version of her paper, the information comes from eight sources: the two cited in her short research paper, two articles from *Family Law Quarterly*, statistics from the Population Reference Bureau, an article from *Black Enterprise*, another from a news information service, and a book written by the associate editor of *New Leader* magazine. The examples from both Weitzman and Anderson-Khleif have been supplanted with one example of a man who was left with only $700, after alimony payment, for the entire year and statistics which show, for instance, that "in the United States only 75 percent of separated or divorced women receive any support at all," "that 40 percent of all divorced women receive less salary then men," and "that 73 percent of all poor working women are located in service or clerical jobs (which pay minimum wage)."

Her paper had a new conclusion, too:

> With all the statistics made available, it's easy to see that after a divorce that a woman is affected much harder in the financial area. They not only have to adapt to a new work market, they also must bear the full brunt of raising the children and taking care of their home. Though there may be some women who do not fit into this category, just as there are some men who are not in the group of financially stable men. Further study needs to be done on behalf of the men, and these studies need to be presented to the public. Men on a whole have a tremendous amount of respect for the way others perceive them and because of this pride they tend not to divulge facts as they really are. There are of coarse exceptions to this also.

> With new laws going into effect all the time, hopefully in the future a system will be worked out that when a couple gets divorced, all will be totally equal: money, housing, rearing of children, and earning ability.

Gone were the personal experience, the "sympathy" for the wife and children, and the "devastation." In their places were "statistics," a call for studies made "on behalf of the men," and a further call for an equal sharing of money, housing, and child rearing as well as equal job opportunities for women. I began to feel uncomfortable about the absence of Ms. L's experience in the paper, for I assumed that I had forced Ms. L to become yet another Griselda. I assumed that Ms. L was like "Simone" in *Women's Ways of Knowing*, the student who had learned that teachers are not interested in personal feelings, that writing was a game, a display of rhetoric (Belenky et al 106). A few months after she submitted the final draft, I asked Ms. L if she would agree to an interview so that we could explore why she had changed her voice in successive drafts of her term paper—even the title had changed from the original "Devastation of Divorce" to

"Financial Effects of Divorce." Ms. L readily agreed, and we met in the conference room of the library where I audiotaped our remarks.

I began by asking Ms. L to talk about her experiences as a writer. In particular, I asked about the kinds of writing required in her high school courses. Ms. L replied:

> We had book reports—this was back in the '60s—a couple of term papers (maybe two thousand words would be the maximum)—some essays, a couple of short stories. I remember in lit class we had to write after reading some stuff, try to come up with our own or use a form that had been set up for us. And in English poetry, the different techniques for different styles, sonnets, limericks—I saved some of the work, but most of the freehand stuff I saved from high school.

Curious as to why Ms. L had saved the "freehand stuff" (television scripts and poetry that she had written that had not been assigned), I asked her to explain how she had chosen which papers to save. She replied:

> I think that it was my own, and somebody didn't say you had to do this; where when I had to do a paper for school, I didn't really—even though I was the one who wrote it—I didn't really deem it as my own quote unquote creation, where anything I wrote as poetry or short stories or along those lines was out of my own imagination, and that's probably why I saved it, knowing that the majority of my school work . . . I guess I really didn't take it seriously; you know how while I was in school, you know because I was told that I had to do them.

At this point in our interview, I asked Ms. L if she would look over her different versions of her term paper and try to recall what she was thinking about when she wrote them. Thoroughly enjoying this interviewing process, she readily agreed to meet with me again a few days later. I expected that when I questioned her about the final version of her term paper she would say that her "real" voice was in the poetry and short stories that she was writing and that she had written the final version of her term paper the way that I had wanted it written, that it was not her own "creation." Surprisingly, Ms. L said something altogether different.

Here is how she explained the final version of her term paper:

> I made up my mind to try to remain unbiased and to put myself away from the paper, and not being in the paper as I had done in the first draft—quoting that I was recently divorced and statistics about myself in there . . . it was sort of as if I didn't really want to share that—not that it isn't known . . . it was just, not that it was too personal, it was just, um, I guess I just didn't feel myself worthy to be put into a paper compared to books that were presented; you know, it was like I was just, I don't know, a minor fraction of it all. . . .

I asked her if it were my comment, "I think you may want to have a more unbiased point of view," that had made her change her approach. And I especially asked her to explain what she had meant by not being "worthy." The following exchange suggests that Ms. L's impersonal voice was carefully chosen and "real." She explained,

> I guess it was, um, (long pause) sort of like I just didn't own up to be interacted with other facts that I had gotten to be put into the paper. I don't know—if I had just dealt with that on a personal level, my own feelings—because all the other facts that I had read . . . though divorce is emotional—were set forth as straight facts without the overtone of the emotion that I had to be put in. I think that's when I did decide to get into the middle of the road and that was when I decided to completely withdraw myself.

I asked Ms. L if she meant that the sources she was looking at were less personal. She agreed:

> Right. Less personal, and I just felt that it would be just too much personal. I think if I was writing an essay about *my own* feelings of divorce, then I would be able to present that and maybe draw in some of the facts that I had researched. And that would be all right. But on a term paper, where I really wanted to stay impersonal. . . . I think that, as a writer, the best I could do is remain completely neutral.

I then asked Ms. L if she felt "voiceless" in her paper.

Oh no, no, no! I put myself into the paper, so my thoughts are in the paper—because your emotions aren't in the paper doesn't mean that you're voiceless. My thoughts are still there, and even though there are still emotions in those thoughts (as in every thought there is), there wasn't that personal emotion of me going through the divorce and just shoving it out on people.

I had misunderstood the changes in the different versions of Ms. L's research paper, but I would not have realized that if I had not engaged Ms. L in a conversation, in the interviews that both she and I enjoyed. Ms. L had not felt that I had co-opted her discourse and had not felt alienated and voiceless in argument. She felt that she had grown as a writer. She had liked her final version of her research paper and, in fact, had declared that given the opportunity, she would have revised other passages that she felt were too emotional. I cautiously conclude that in her conversation with her sources, she gained new skills, "an ability to empathize with, yet judge" (Flynn, "Gender" 286). I do not intend Ms. L's case to be viewed as a representative case, but she is one example of an inexperienced writer who, in becoming more attuned to the voices adopted in the discourses of the arts and sciences, found a "worthy" voice, a voice that is likely to stand her well in the other discourses in which she must write. I spoke with Ms. L again about a year after we had completed our interviews. She is now studying to become a paralegal, and her fellow students are encouraging her to become a lawyer. She "sounds" like one, they say.

WHAT TO DO? WHAT TO DO?

At the conclusion of the review essay whose questions provide the opening questions of this study, Patricia Bizzell observes that J. Elspeth Stuckey's *The Violence of Literacy*

calls the bluff of all of us academics who are interested in talking about literacy, who hope somehow by such talk to evoke social and political connections in our work, because she argues so forcefully that we cannot translate these allu-

sions into reality until that unjust reality changes. ("Professing" 321)

In order to analyze our collective identity crisis, Bizzell says,
we English teachers will have to "talk about how we feel and
what we are going to do" (321).

"What to do? What to do?" June Jordan asked in her
keynote address to the National Council of Teachers of
English meeting in 1982 (Stuckey 97). Jordan's questions provide a refrain for the litany of wrongheaded assumptions
about the efficacy of literacy instruction that Stuckey intones
in her aptly titled "The Violence of Literacy"chapter. My
view of literacy is a more hopeful one than Stuckey's. Like
Thomas Fox, I find that "we need not get depressed about
the enormity of the changes necessary to make education
transformative" (119). What to do? I look to Bleich's definition of literacy as "an inquiry into how to say what matters to
other people that matter" as a starting point (*Double* 330) and
to Robinson's metaphor of "novelized languages" to describe
the nature of our talk about literacy (321). Although I want
our talk of literacy to begin with our students in our classrooms, I want it to go beyond our classrooms and beyond
compartments in the field of composition; we must engage in
conversations with the communities outside our academic
communities as well. For example, if our colleagues in the
secondary schools ask for our help in defining "national"
standards, we have to accept their invitations to converse.

In our classrooms, I have argued for the acceptance
of multiple literacies. As students from different cultures
increasingly find their way into our composition classrooms,
I am suggesting that we English teachers should open our
classrooms not only to the logic of non-conventional writing
(in the spirit of Shaughnessy's *Errors and Expectations*) but to
the logic of non-conventional reading as well. It is important
that we study the class, gender, and cultural backgrounds that
generate these interpretations, paying particular attention
to where these factors intersect. To accomplish that goal,
we need to know a great deal about the literacies that our
students bring with them to our classrooms. Hull and Rose's

case studies, their micro-level close examinations of oral and written discourse in remedial classrooms, can provide much of that information. The field needs more studies like theirs, especially in that neglected space, the non-remedial classroom in the non-competitive college or university. "Practitioner's lore" can provide us with many of those insights. I am thinking especially of Joan Wauters's discovery that Native American students respond positively to structured, non-confrontational collaborative groups. But I wonder why I had to learn of her insight in the work of Terry Dean (32). I am hopeful that the journals in the profession are truly more open now to the novelized languages that marginalized practitioners often speak. Finally, we must be as open to transformation as we hope that our students will become. Our students' desires for vocational skills must not always be perceived as a problem to be solved. As Villanueva has cogently argued, "Freirestas" tend to forget that they do not have the right to deny their students' desires for vocational skills, the keys, in their students' minds, to the American dream (258).

It is important, too, that we English teachers converse with those in different disciplines. Recognizing that written language is acquired through actual use and thereby governed by cultural conventions, we should encourage ethnographic studies into the cultures that our students bring with them into the classroom and make ourselves aware of their findings. Joanna Street and Brian Street argue that research must begin from a conception of literacy "as the *social* practice of reading and writing" that "eschews value judgments about the relative superiority of schooled literacies over other literacies" (148). Carole Edelsky calls for research that will make us aware not only of the ways written products are treated in different languages but also of the consequences of being able to write in different languages (49). Hull and her coauthors seek to forge links between the micro-analyses of classroom conversation and writing and the macro-analyses of society and culture in order "to provide a richer understanding of the history and logic of particular behaviors" ("Remediation" 323). Above all, as we make forays into these other fields, we must remember that premises are assailable.

Of course no amount of ethnographic research will ever account for the almost dizzying complexities of the diversity of cultures we English teachers will be exposed to. I can propose no single solution to the chilliness that so many non-Western, non-mainstream students feel in composition classrooms. How could any research ever keep up with it all? Our conversations must include our students as well. I never would have understood what really happened in Ms. L's research paper had I not interviewed her about it.

Most importantly, we English teachers must not lose sight of the politics of all discussions about language use and language instruction. As classrooms in American colleges and universities become increasingly diverse and funds for higher education shrink, discussions of access and excellence will become questions of access or excellence. We are in the forefront of those discussions, and their outcomes are of tremendous importance to our students. In the words of Henry Giroux, we must become teachers who "make a difference"; we must have "the courage to take risks, to look into the future, and to imagine a world that could be opposed to simply what is" (*Schooling* 215).

Notes

1. By the time the weekend following a big news event has passed, people are ready to move on to something else (Royko B6).

2. By 1990, 13 million students were enrolled in institutions of higher learning; in fact, 32.5 percent of all white 18- to 24-year-olds, 25.4 percent of all African American 18- to 24-year-olds, and 15.8 percent of all Hispanic 18- to 24-year-olds were enrolled in college (American 8).

3. Nancy Sommers's dissertation, "Revision in the Composing Process: A Case Study of College Freshmen and Experienced Adult Writers," and Linda Flower's *Problem-Solving Strategies for Writing* are representative studies of this sort.

4. For an account of the vitriolic tenor of these attacks, see Cheryl Geisler's "Exploring Academic Literacy: An Experiment in Composing" or Stephen M. North's *The Making of Knowledge in Composition*, 260–62, 270–71.

5. Terry Dean declares that "cultural dissonance" plays an important role in dropout rates. Until the institution of the Puente Project in California, 50 to 60 percent of Chicano and Latino students enrolled in fifteen California community colleges dropped out during their first year (24, 31). Gregory Glau attributes an even higher dropout rate (or perhaps, "stopout" rate) of Native American students to "classroom discomfort"; only 6 percent of those Native Americans who enroll in college graduate (51).

6. Several of these studies are from the field of contrastive rhetoric, identified with a positivistic "current-traditional" approach to writing instruction. Despite my insistence on the importance of a social constructionist approach to writing instruction, I find the field's studies of Japanese, Chinese, and Spanish

languages instructive, particularly in light of the fact that a growing number of students have had early schooling in other countries. Some critics challenge contrastive rhetoricians' notion that the "temperament" of a culture accounts for the ways that writers from that culture compose. However, since most writing instruction occurs in schools, and since schools are sites for cultural reproduction, it stands to reason that the preferred discourse style of the school is a reflection of the values of the culture that the school reproduces.

Works Cited

Allaei, Sara Kurtz and Ulla Maija Connor. "Exploring the Dynamics of Cross-Cultural Collaboration in Writing Classrooms." *The Writing Instructor* 10 (1990): 19–28.

Allen, Diane. "Bridging Cultures for College Students: Minority Faculty Help." *The Council Chronicle* Apr. 1992: 1+.

Altman, Meryl. "How Not to Do Things with Metaphors We Live By." *College English* 52 (1990): 495–506.

American Council on Education. *Tenth Annual Status Report on Minorities in Higher Education* (1991). Washington: American Council on Education, 1992.

"Analyzing Talk, Tannen Promotes Understanding between Sexes." *The Council Chronicle* Feb. 1992: 8.

Annas, Pamela J. "Silences: Feminist Language Research and the Teaching of Writing." Caywood and Overing. 3–17.

———. "Style as Politics: A Feminist Approach to the Teaching of Writing." *College English* 47 (1985): 360–71.

Anson, Chris M., and Hildy Miller. "Journals in Composition: An Update." *College Composition and Communication* 39 (1988): 198–216.

Armstrong, Cherryl. "Reexamining Basic Writers: Lessons from Harvard's Basic Writers." *Journal of Basic Writing* 7 (1988): 68–80.

Arnove, Robert F., and Harvey J. Graff, eds. Introduction. *National Literacy Campaigns: Historical and Comparative Perspectives*. New York: Plenum, 1987.

Ashton-Jones, Evelyn. "Collaboration, Conversation, and the Politics of Gender." Unpublished manuscript, 1992.

Ashton-Jones, Evelyn, and Dene Kay Thomas. "Composition, Collaboration, and Women's Ways of Knowing: A Conversation with Mary Belenky." *Journal of Advanced Composition* 10 (1990): 275–92.

Bartholomae, David. "Inventing the University." Kintgen, Kroll, and Rose. 273–85.

Bartholomae, David, and Anthony R. Petrosky. *Facts Artifacts and Counterfacts.* Upper Montclair, NJ: Boynton, 1986.

Basso, K. H. " 'To Give up on Words': Silence in Western Apache Culture." *Language and Social Context.* Ed. Pier Paolo Giglioi. London: Cox, 1972. 67–86.

Bazerman, Charles. "A Relationship between Reading and Writing: The Conversational Model." *College English* 41 (1980): 656–61.

———. Rev. of *Reading-to-Write: Exploring a Cognitive Process,* by Linda Flower, Victoria Stein, John Ackerman, Margaret J. Kantz, Kathleen McCormick, and Wayne C. Peck. *Journal of Advanced Composition* 12 (1992): 236–42.

Belenky, Mary, et al. *Women's Ways of Knowing: The Development of Self, Voice, and Mind.* New York: Basic, 1986.

Berlin, James A. *Writing Instruction in Nineteenth-Century American Colleges.* Carbondale: Southern Illinois UP, 1984.

Bizzell, Patricia. *Academic Discourse and Critical Consciousness.* Pittsburgh: U of Pittsburgh P, 1992.

———. "Arguing about Literacy." *College English* 50 (1988): 141–53.

———. "Beyond Anti-Foundationalism to Rhetorical Authority: Problems Defining 'Cultural Literacy.' " *College English* 52 (1990): 661–75.

———. "Cognition, Convention, and Certainty: What We Need to Know about Writing." *Pre/Text* 3 (1982): 214–43.

———. "College Composition: Initiation into the Academic Discourse Community." *Curriculum Inquiry* 12 (1982): 191–207.

———. "Professing Literacy: A Review Essay." *Journal of Advanced Composition* 11 (1991): 315–22.

———. "What Happens When Basic Writers Come to College?" *College Composition and Communication* 37 (1986): 294–301.

Bleich, David. *The Double Perspective: Language, Literacy, and Social Relations.* New York: Oxford UP, 1988.

———. "Sexism in Academic Styles of Learning." *Journal of Advanced Composition* 10 (1990): 231–47.

Bloom, Allan. *The Closing of the American Mind: How Higher Education Has Failed Democracy and Impoverished the Souls of Today's Students.* New York: Simon, 1987.

Bogdan, Deanne, and Stanley B. Straw, eds. *Beyond Communication: Reading Comprehension and Criticism.* Portsmouth, NH: Boynton, 1990.

Booth, Wayne. Foreword. *The English Coalition Conference: Democracy through Language.* Ed. Richard Lloyd-Jones and Andrea Lunsford. Urbana: NCTE, 1989.

Bourdieu, Pierre, and J. P. Passeron. *Reproduction in Education, Society, and Culture.* Beverly Hills: Sage, 1977.

Boyd, Richard. "Imitate Me; Don't Imitate Me: Mimeticism in David Bartholomae's 'Inventing the University.'" *Journal of Advanced Composition* 11 (1991): 335–45.

Brewer, William F. Letter. *The Nation* 63 (1896): 327.

Brodkey, Linda. "On the Subjects of Class and Gender in 'The Literacy Letters.'" *College English* 51 (1989): 125–41.

Bruffee, Kenneth A. "Collaborative Learning and the 'Conversation of Mankind.'" *College English* 46 (1984): 635–52.

———. "Peer Tutoring and the 'Conversation of Mankind.'" *Writing Centers: Theory and Administration.* Ed. Gary A. Olson. Urbana: NCTE, 1984.

Bullock, Richard, and John Trimbur, eds. *The Politics of Writing Instruction: Postsecondary.* Portsmouth, NH: Boynton, 1991.

Burke, Kenneth. *The Philosophy of Literary Form: Studies in Symbolic Action.* 2nd ed. Baton Rouge: Louisiana State UP, 1967.

Cameron, Deborah, Fiona McAlinden, and Kathy O'Leary. "Gossip Revisited: Language in All-Female Groups." Coates and Cameron. 94–122.

Carroll, John B., and Jeanne S. Chall. "Report of the Committee on Reading, National Academy of Education." *Toward a Literate Society: The Report of the Committee on Reading of the National Academy of Education.* New York: McGraw, 1975. 3–57.

Cayton, Mary Kupiec. "What Happens When Things Go Wrong: Women and Writing Blocks." *Journal of Advanced Composition* 10 (1990): 321–37.

———. "Writing as Outsiders: Academic Discourse and Marginalized Faculty." *College English* 53 (1991): 647–60.

Caywood, Cynthia L., and Gillian R. Overing. *Teaching Writing: Pedagogy, Gender, and Equity.* Albany: State U of New York P, 1987.

Chodorow, Nancy. *The Reproduction of Mothering: Psychoanalysis and the Sociology of Gender.* Berkeley: U of California P, 1978.

Clifford, John. Rev. of *Cognitive Processes of Writing.* Ed. Lee W. Gregg and Erwin R. Steinberg. *College Composition and Communication* 34 (1983): 99–101.

Coates, Jennifer. Introduction. Coates and Cameron. 64–73.

Coates, Jennifer, and Deborah Cameron, eds. *Women in Their Speech Communities: New Perspectives on Language and Sex.* London: Longman, 1988.

College of the Holy Cross Catalog. 1991–1992. Worcester, MA: College of the Holy Cross, 1991.

Collins, Patricia Hill. *Black Feminist Thought: Knowledge, Consciousness, and Politics of Empowerment.* New York: Routledge, 1991.

Connors, Robert J. "Composition Studies and Science." *College English* 45 (1983): 1–20.

Cooper, Marilyn M. "Dueling with Dualism: A Response to Interviews with Mary Field Belenky and Gayatri Chakravorty Spivak." *Journal of Advanced Composition* 11 (1991): 179–85.

———. "Unhappy Consciousness in First-Year English: How to Figure Things Out for Yourself." Cooper and Holzman, "Writing" 28–60.

———. "Women's Ways of Writing." Cooper and Holzman, "Writing" 141–56.

Cooper, Marilyn M., and Michael Holzman. "Talking about Protocols." *College Composition and Communication* 34 (1983): 284–93.

———. *Writing as a Social Action.* Portsmouth, NH: Boynton, 1989.

Coy, Edward G. Letter. *The Nation* 63 (1896): 344.

Crawford, Mary, and Roger Chaffin. "The Researcher's Construction of Meaning: Cognitive Research on Gender and Comprehension." Flynn and Schweickart. 3–30.

Curtiss, Elmer L. Letter. *The Nation* 63 (1896): 420–21.

Daniels, Harvey A. *Famous Last Words: The American Language Crisis Reconsidered.* Carbondale: Southern Illinois UP, 1983.

Daumer, Elisabeth, and Sandra Runzo. "Transforming the Composition Classroom." Caywood and Overing. 45–62.

Dean, Terry. "Multicultural Classrooms, Monocultural Teachers." *College Composition and Communication* 40 (1989): 23–37.

Edelsky, Carole. *With Literacy and Justice for All: Rethinking the Social in Language and Education.* Critical Perspectives on Literacy and Education. London: Falmer, 1991.

Edwards, Audrey. "Fighting Racism: Join the Movement to Spark a New Age of Tolerance." *American Express Card Connections* Winter 1992: 12–15.

Elbow, Peter. "Reflections on Academic Discourse: How It Relates to Freshmen Colleagues." *College English* 53 (1991): 135–55.

———. *What Is English?* New York: MLA, 1990.

Ellis, Donald. Letter. *Chronicle of Higher Education* 31 July 1991: B2.

Elson, John. "Campus of the Future." *Time* 13 Apr. 1992: 54–58.

Enos, Theresa. *A Sourcebook for Basic Writing Teachers.* New York: Random, 1987.

"Facts on File: 1991–1992 Tuition Fees at More than 2,900 Colleges and Universities." *Chronicle of Higher Education* 23 Oct. 1991: A31–36.

Finn, Chester E., Jr. *We Must Take Charge: Our Schools and Our Future.* New York: Free, 1991.

Fishman, Pamela M. "Interaction: The Work Women Do." Thorne, Kramarae, and Henley. 89–101.

Flower, Linda. *Problem Solving Strategies for Writing.* 2nd ed. San Diego: Harcourt, 1985.

———. "Revising Writer-Based Prose." *Journal of Basic Writing* 3 (1981): 62–74.

Flower, Linda, et al. *Reading-to-Write: Exploring a Cognitive and Social Process.* New York: Oxford UP, 1990.

Flynn, Elizabeth A. "Composing as a Woman." *College Composition and Communication* 39 (1988): 423–35.

———. "Composing 'Composing as a Woman': A Perspective on Research." *College Composition and Communication* 41 (1990): 83–91.

———. "Composition Studies from a Feminist Perspective." Bullock and Trimbur. 137–54.

———. "Gender and Reading." Flynn and Schweickart. 267–88.

———. "Politicizing the Composing Process and Women's Ways of Interacting: A Response to 'A Conversation with Mary Belenky.'" *Journal of Advanced Composition* 11 (1991): 173–78.

———. Rev. of *The Gender Reader*, ed. Evelyn Ashton-Jones and Gary A. Olson. *Journal of Advanced Composition* 12 (1992): 223–25.

Flynn, Elizabeth A, and Patrocinio P. Schweickart, eds. *Gender and Reading: Essays on Readers, Texts, and Contexts.* Baltimore: Johns Hopkins UP, 1986.

Fontaine, Sheryl I., and Susan Hunter, eds. *Writing Ourselves into the Story: Unheard Voices from Composition Studies.* Carbondale: Southern Illinois UP, 1993.

Fontaine, Sheryl I., John Peavoy, and Susan Hunter. "Underprivileged Voices in the Academy of the Privileged." *Freshman English News* 19 (1990): 2–9.

"Foreign Students in the U.S." *Chronicle of Higher Education* 23 Oct. 1991: A1+.

Fox, Thomas J. *The Social Uses of Writing: Politics and Pedagogy.* Norwood, NJ: Ablex, 1990.

Franklin, Phyllis. "From the Editor." *Profession 91.* New York: MLA, 1991 1–4.

Freire, Paulo. "The Adult Literacy Process as Cultural Action for Freedom and Education and Conscientizaçao." Kintgen, Kroll, and Rose. 398–409.

———. *Pedagogy of the Oppressed.* Trans. Myrna Bergman Ramos. New York: Seabury, 1970.

Fricke, Philip K., and Diane M. Shand. "General Motors Update."*Prudential Securities Research* 9 July 1993.

Gailliot, Henry J. "Cycles of History and the 1990s." *Economic & Market Review* 15.2 (1993).

Gebhardt, Richard. "Editor's Notes." *College Composition and Communication* 42 (1991): 9–10.

Geisler, Cheryl. "Exploring Academic Literacy: An Experiment in Composing." *College Composition and Cummunication* 43 (1992): 39–54.

———. "Towards a Sociocognitive Model of Literacy: Constructing Mental Models in a Philosophical Conversation." *Textual Dynamics of the Professions: Historical and Contemporary Studies of Writing in Professional Communities.* Eds. Charles Bazerman and James Paradis. Madison: U of Wisconsin P, 1991.

Gilligan, Carol. *In a Different Voice: Psychological Theory and Women's Development.* Cambridge, MA: Harvard UP, 1982.

Gilyard, Keith. *Voices of the Self: A Study of Language Competence.* Detroit: Wayne State UP, 1991.

Girout, Henry A. *Schooling and the Struggle for Public Life: Critical Pedagogy in the Modern Age.* American Culture Series. Minneapolis: U of Minnesota P, 1988.

———. *Teachers as Intellectuals: Toward a Critical Pedagogy of Learning*. Critical Studies in Education Series. Granby, MA: Bergin, 1988.

Glau, Gregory R. "Returning Power: Native American Classroom (Dis)Comfort & Effective Communication." *The Writing Instructor* 10 (1990): 51–58.

Goulston, Wendy. "Women Writing." Caywood and Overing. 19–29.

Graff, Harvey J. *The Literacy Myth: Literature and Social Structure in The Nineteenth-Century City*. New York: Academic, 1979.

Grantham, Shelby. "Johnny Can't Write? Who Cares?" *Dartmouth Alumni Magazine* Jan. 1977: 20–22.

"The Growing Illiteracy of American Boys." *The Nation* 63 (1896): 284–85.

Grumet, Madeleine R. *Bitter Milk*. Amherst: U of Massachusetts P, 1988.

Henning, Barbara. "The World Was Stone Cold: Basic Writing in an Urban University." *College English* 53 (1991): 674–85.

Herzberg, Bruce. "Composition and the Politics of the Curriculum." Bullock and Trimbur. 277–95.

Hirsch, E. D., Jr. "Cultural Literacy Does Not Mean a List of Works." *ADE Bulletin* 84 (1986): 1–3.

———. *Cultural Literacy: What Every American Needs to Know*. Boston: Houghton, 1987.

Holzman, Michael. "The Social Context of Literacy." Cooper and Holzman. 133–40.

Hood, Wayne, and Dina Pilotis. "Sears, Roebuck and Co. Company Update." *Prudential Securities Research* 23 Feb. 1993.

House, Ernest R., Carol Emmer, and Nancy Lawrence. "Cultural Literacy Reconsidered." *Literacy for a Diverse Society: Perspectives, Practices, and Policies*. Ed. Elfrieda H. Hiebert. New York: Teachers College P, 1991. 58–74.

"How to Build Up a University." *The Nation* 63 (1896): 494–95.

Hull, Glynda, and Mike Rose. "Rethinking Remediation: Toward a Social Cognitive Understanding of Problematic Reading and Writing." *Written Communication* 6 (1989): 139–54.

———. " 'This Wooden Shack Place': The Logic of an Unconventional Reading." *College Composition and Communication* 41 (1990): 287–98.

Hull, Glynda, et al. "Remediation as a Social Construct: Perspectives from an Analysis of Classroom Discourse." *College Composition and Communication* 42 (1991): 299–329.

Hunter, Carman St. John, and David Harman. *Adult Illiteracy in the United States.* New York: McGraw, 1985.

Hunter, Susan. "The Dangers of Teaching Differently." Fontaine and Hunter. 70–85.

———. "A Woman's Place *Is* in the Composition Classroom: Pedagogy, Gender, and Difference." *Rhetoric Review* 9 (1991): 230–45.

Kaestle, Carl F., et al. *Literacy and Reading since 1880.* New Haven: Yale UP, 1991.

Kaplan, Robert B. "Writing in a Multilingual/Multicultural Context: What's Contrastive about Contrastive Rhetoric?" *The Writing Instructor* 10 (1990): 7–17.

Kerr, Clark. *The Great Transformation in Higher Education, 1960–1980.* Frontiers in Education Series. Albany: State U of New York P, 1991.

Kintgen, Eugene R., Barry M. Kroll, and Mike Rose, eds. *Perspectives in Literacy.* Carbondale: Southern Illinois UP, 1988.

Kitzhaber, Albert R. *Rhetoric in American Colleges: 1850–1900.* Dallas: Southern Methodist UP, 1990.

Kraemer, Don. "Enthymemes and Feminist Discourse: Mediating Public and Private Identity." *Freshman English News* 19 (1990): 37–40.

———. "No Exit: A Play of Literacy and Gender." *Journal of Advanced Composition* 10 (1990): 305–19.

Kroll, Keith. "Building Communities: Joining the Community of Professional Teachers." *Teaching English in the Two-Year College* 17 (1990). 103–8.

Laditka, James N. "Semiology, Ideology, and *Praxis*: Responsible Authority in the Composition Classroom." *Journal of Advanced Composition* 10 (1990): 357–73.

Lakoff, Robin. *Language and Woman's Place*. New York: Harper, 1975.

———. *Talking Power: The Politics of Language in Our Lives*. New York: Basic, 1990.

Lamb, Catherine E. "Beyond Argument in Feminist Composition." *College Composition and Communication* 42 (1991): 11–24.

Laurence, Patricia. Letter: *Chronicle of Higher Education* 31 July 1991: B2.

Lazere, Donald. "Back to Basics: A Force for Oppression or Liberation?" *College English* 54 (1992): 7–21.

———. "Orality, Literacy, and Standard English." *Journal of Basic Writing* 10 (1991): 87–98.

Lloyd-Jones, Richard, and Andrea A. Lunsford, eds. *The English Coalition Conference: Democracy Through Language*. Urbana: NCTE, 1989.

Lu, Min-zhan. "From Silence to Words: Writing as Struggle." *College English* 49 (1987): 437–48.

———. "Redefining the Legacy of Mina Shaughnessy: A Critique of the Politics of Innocence." *Journal of Basic Writing* 10 (1991): 26–40.

Lunsford, Andrea. "Politics and Practice in Basic Writing." Enos. 246–58.

Lunsford, Andrea, and Particia A. Sullivan. "Who Are Basic Writers?" Moran and Jacobi. 17–30.

Mao, LuMing. "Persuasion, Cooperation and Diversity of Rhetorics." *Rhetoric Society Quarterly* 20 (1990): 131–42.

Matalene, Carolyn. "Contrastive Rhetoric: An American Writing Teacher in China." *College English* 47 (1985): 789–808.

McCracken, Nancy Miller, Lois I. Green, and Claudia M. Greenwood. "Gender in Composition Research: A Strange Silence." Fontaine and Hunter. 352–73.

Middleton, Joyce Irene. Rev. of *The Double Perspective* by David Bleich. *College Composition and Communication* 41 (1990): 231–33.

Miller, Susan. *Textual Carnivals: The Politics of Composition.* Carbondale: Southern Illinois UP, 1991.

Moran, Michael, and Martin Jacobi. *Research in Basic Writing.* New York: Greenwood, 1990.

National Commission on Excellence in Education. *A Nation at Risk: The Imperative for Educational Reform.* Washington: U.S. Department of Education, 1983.

North, Stephen. *The Making of Knowledge in Composition: Portrait of an Emerging Field.* Portsmouth, NH: Boynton, 1987.

Ogbu, John. "Cultural Diversity and School Experience." Walsh. 25–50.

Ohmann, Richard. Foreword. Bullock and Trimbur. ix–xvi.

———. *The Politics of Letters.* Middleton, CT: Wesleyan UP, 1987.

Pearlman, Mickey. "How I Would Liberate My Mother." Caywood and Overing. 165–68.

Pennycook, Alastair. "The Concept of Method, Interested Knowledge, and the Politics of Language Teaching." *TESOL Quarterly* 23 (1989): 589–618.

Perry, Donna M. "Making Journal Writing Matter." Caywood and Overing. 151–56.

Peterson's Competitive Colleges: 1991–92. 10th ed. Princeton, NJ: Peterson's Guides, 1991.

Piatek, Doris M. Rev. of *The Gender Reader,* ed. Evelyn Ashton-Jones and Gary A. Olson. *Teaching English in the Two-Year College* 19 (1992): 69–70.

Raines, Helon Howell. "Is There a Writing Program in This College?: Two Hundred and Thirty-six Two-Year Schools Respond." *College Composition and Communication* 41 (1990): 151–65.

Riemer, James D. "Becoming Gender Conscious: Writing about Sex Roles in a Composition Course." Caywood and Overing. 157–68.

Roberts, Edgar V., and Henry E. Jacobs. *Literature: An Introduction to Reading and Writing.* 2nd ed. Englewood Cliffs, NJ: Prentice, 1989.

Robinson, Jay L., ed. *Conversations on the Written Word: Essays on Language and Literacy.* Portsmouth, NH: Boynton, 1990.

———. "The Wall of Babel; Or, Up Against the Language Barrier." Robinson. 53–91.

Rose, Mike. "The Language of Exclusion: Writing Instruction at the University. *College English* 47 (1985): 431–59.

———. *Lives on the Boundary: The Struggles and Achievements of America's Underprepared.* New York: Free, 1989.

———. "Narrowing the Mind and the Page." *College Composition and Communication* 39 (1988): 267–302.

———. "Remedial Writing Courses: A Critique and a Proposal." Enos. 104–24.

Royko, Mike. "The Fire Is Going Out of the L. A. Riot Story." *Las Vegas Review-Journal* 13 May 1992, final ed.: B6.

Ruddick, Sara. *Maternal Thinking.* Boston: Beacon, 1989.

Russell David R. *Writing in the Academic Disciplines, 1870–1990: A Curricular History.* Carbondale: Southern Illinois UP, 1991.

St. Petersburg Junior College Catalog. 1987–1988. St. Petersburg, FL: St. Petersburg Junior College, 1987.

Schriner, Delores K., and Matthew Willen. "The Facts on *Facts*: Adaptations to a Reading and Writing Course." *College Composition and Communication* 42 (1991): 230–38.

Scollon, Ron, and Suzanne B. K. Scollon. *Narrative, Literacy, and Face in Interethnic Communication.* Advances in Discourse Processes 7. Norwood, NJ: Ablex, 1981.

Shaughnessy, Mina P. *Errors and Expectations: A Guide for the Teacher of Basic Writing.* New York: Oxford UP, 1977.

Sheils, Merrill. "Why Johnny Can't Write." *Newsweek* 8 Dec. 1975: 58–65.

Shen, Fan. "The Classroom and the Wider Culture: Identity as a Key to Learning English Composition. *College Composition and Communication* 40 (1989): 459–66.

Sommers, Nancy. "Revision in the Composing Process: A Case Study of College Freshmen and Experienced Adult Writers." Diss. Boston U, 1978.

Stanback, Marsha Houston. "What Makes Scholarship about Black Women and Communication Feminist Communication Scholarship?" *Women's Studies in Communication* 11 (1988): 28–31.

Stanger, Carol. "The Sexual Politics of the One-to-One Tutorial Approach and Collaborative Learning." Caywood and Overing 31–44.

Stedman, Lawrence C., and Carl F. Kaestle. "Literacy and Reading Performance in the United States from 1880 to the Present." Kaestle, et al. 75–128.

Stevens, Edward, Jr. "The Anatomy of Mass Literacy in Nineteenth-Century United States." Arnove and Graff. 99–122.

Stewart, Donald C. "Responses to Catherine E. Lamb, 'Beyond Argument in Feminist Composition.' " *College Composition and Communication* 42 (1991): 496–97.

Street, Joanna C., and Brian V. Street. "The Schooling of Literacy." *Writing in the Community*. Ed. David Barton and Roz Ivanic. San Francisco: Sage, 1991. 143–66.

Stuckey, J. Elspeth. *The Violence of Literacy*. Portsmouth, NH: Boynton: 1991.

Swann, Joan. "Talk Control: An Illustration from the Classroom of Problems in Analysing Male Dominance of Conversation." Coates and Cameron. 123–40.

Tannen, Deborah. "Teachers' Classroom Strategies Should Recognize that Men and Women Use Language Differently." *Chronicle of Higher Education* 19 June 1991: B1+.

———. *You Just Don't Understand: Women and Men in Conversation*. New York: Morrow, 1990.

Thomas, Gordon P. Rev. of *The Social Uses of Writing: Politics and Pedagogy*, by Thomas Fox. *Journal of Advanced Composition* 11 (1991): 220–23.

Thorne, Barrie, Cheris Kramarae, and Nancy Henley. *Language, Gender, and Society*. Rowley, MA: Newbury, 1983.

Tinberg, Howard B. " 'An Enlargement of Observation': More on Theory Building in the Composition Classroom." *College Composition and Communication* 42 (1991): 36–44.

Troyka, Lynn Q. "Defining Basic Writers in Context." Enos. 2–15.

———. "Perspectives on Legacies and Literacy in the 1980s." *College Composition and Communication* 33 (1982): 252–62.

Tuman, Myron. *A Preface to Literacy: An Inquiry into Pedagogy, Practice, and Progress.* Tuscaloosa: U of Alabama P, 1987.

University of Pittsburgh Bulletin (1989–1991). Pittsburgh, PA: Department of University Relations, 1989.

Valdés, Guadalupe. "Bilingual Minorities and Language Issues in Writing." *Written Communication* 9 (1992): 85–136.

Veysey, Laurence R. *The Emergence of the American University.* Chicago: U of Chicago P, 1965.

Villanueva, Victor. "Considerations for American Freirestas." Bullock and Trimbur. 247–62.

Wall, Susan, and Nicholas Coles. "Reading Basic Writing: Alternatives to a Pedagogy of Accommodation." Bullock and Trimbur. 227–46.

Walsh, Catherine, ed. *Literacy as Praxis: Culture, Language and Pedagogy.* Norwood, NJ: Ablex, 1991.

Watanabe, Teresa. "Japanese Leaders Rap U.S. Workers." *Las Vegas Review-Journal* 21 Jan. 1992, final ed.: A1+.

West, Candace, and Don Zimmerman. "Small Insults: A Study of Interruptions in Cross-Sex Conversations between Unacquainted Persons." Thorne, Kramarae, and Henley. 102–17.

"Why Johnny Can't Write—And What's Being Done." *U.S. News and World Report* 16 Mar. 1981: 47–48.

Willinsky, John. *The New Literacy: Redefining Reading and Writing in the Schools.* New York: Routledge, 1990.

Wolk, Marianne. "International Business Machines Report Preview." *Prudential Securities Research Alert.* 14 Dec. 1992.

Woods, Nicola. "Talking Shop: Sex and Status as Determinants of Floor Apportionment in a Work Setting." Coates and Cameron. 141–57.

Zook, Jim. "10 Years Later, Educators See Little Progress for the 'Nation at Risk.' " *The Chronicle of Higher Education* 21 Apr. 1993: A19+.

Index

A

Academic Discourse: and basic
  writers 23–52; conventions,
  17; definition of, xv;
  influence of class on, 38;
  Eurocentrism, 71; feminist
  critique of, 43, 55, 56–61;
  masculinist, 42, 56, 58, 65–66
Adler, Mortimer, 80
Allaei, Sara Kurtz, 91
Altman, Meryl, 67
Annas, Pamela, 62, 70
Argument, as critical literacy,
  xiv–xv, 39–40
Armstrong, Cherryl, 35, 36
Ashton-Jones, Evelyn, 66, 70,
  93

B

Bartholomae, David, 31, 36;
  *Facts, Artifacts, and
  Counterfacts*, 29, 34, 36, 101;
  "Inventing the University,"
  25, 28
Basic writers, definition of, 23,
  24, 27, 30, 35–36, 39
Basic writing, in two-year
  colleges, 37–38; influence of

class on, 34; pedagogy,
  101–102, 104
Basso, K. H., 93
Bazerman, Charles, 101,
  105–106
Belenky, Mary, 66. *See also
  Women's Ways of Knowing*
Berlin, James, 8–9
Bilingual students, 84
Bizzell, Patricia, 17, 28, 31, 36,
  80; *Academic Discourse and
  Critical Consciousness*, 40;
  "Arguing about Literacy,"
  28, "Beyond Anti-
  Foundationalism," 18, 19, 25,
  28; "Cognition, Convention,
  and Certainty," 17; "College
  Composition," 27–28;
  "Professing Literacy," xiii,
  40, 124–25; "What Happens
  When Basic Writers Come to
  College," 17, 40
Bleich, David, 39; *The Double
  Perspective*, 42–43, 56–57,
  107; "Sexism in Academic
  Styles of Learning," 54
Bloom, Allan, xiv, 80
Booth, Wayne, 18
Bourdieu, Pierre, 89
Brodkey, Linda, 73–74
Bruffee, Kenneth, 106

Kramarae, Cheris, 59
Kroll, Keith, 37–38

L

Labov, William, 59
Laditka, James N., 58
"Lakoff Hypothesis," 59–60
Lakoff, Robin, 53, 59, 60, 67, 69
Lamb, Catherine, 67
Language use: cultural aspects of, 77–99; effects of class on, 44–52, 54; social aspects of, 30; masculinist, 54, 56, 58
Lawrence, Nancy, 10, 77–78
Lazere, Donald, 20, 40, 47, 49–50
Literacy: class aspects of, 38, 44–52, 74; critical, 42; cultural aspects of, xiv, 15–16, 50–51, 79; definition, xiv, 21; economic aspects of, 78–79, 80, 81; feminist critique of, 65–66; gender aspects of, 74; social aspects of, 9, 21–22, 30, 42. *See also* Cultural literacy
Literacy crisis: at Dartmouth, 13–14; economic aspects of, 10; in nineteenth century, 6–9; in twentieth century, xiii–xv, 9–20; at Yale, 13
Lu, Min-zhan, 29–30, 84–87
Lunsford, Andrea, 30, 35

M

Mao, LuMing, 88–89
Matalene, Carolyn, 87–89
McAlinden, Fiona, 69

Michigan Technological University, 63–64, 71
Moran, Michael, 25, 35
Multicultural classrooms, 83–86; feminist pedagogy in, 83, 86–97; writing instruction in, 71–72. *See also* Interethnic communication

N

Nation at Risk, 9–10
National Council of Teachers of English, 80, 81, 82
North, Stephen, 55
Northern Arizona University, 101–102

O

Ogbu, John, 97
Ohmann, Richard, xiv, 14, 15, 22, 51
O'Leary, Kathy, 69
Oral interaction, cross-cultural differences in, 92–93
Overing, Gillian, 91. *See also* *Teaching Writing: Pedagogy, Gender, and Equity*

P

Peavoy, John, 41, 47–48
Pennycook, Alastair, 82
Perry, Donna M., 62, 71, 103
Perry, William, 58–59
Petrosky, Arthur R., *Facts, Artifacts, and Counterfacts*, 29, 34, 36, 101

nineteenth century, 7–8;
twentieth century, 10–11
University of California, Davis,
83
University of California, Los
Angeles, 32–33, 34
University of Nevada, Las
Vegas, 83
University of Pittsburgh, 33–34
U.S. News and World Report,
14

V

Valdés, Guadalupe, 82
Villanueva, Victor, 40, 102

W

Wall, Susan, 34–35, 41
Warnock, John, 21
West, Candace, 59, 60, 61, 68
"Why Johnny Can't Write,"

xiii, 12–13
"Why Johnny Can't Write—and
What's Being Done," 14
Women's Ways of Knowing
(Belenky, Clinchy,
Goldberger, and Tarule), 56,
58–59, 63, 65, 121
"Women's Ways of Writing"
(Cooper), 63, 67
Woods, Nicola, 69
Writing instruction: for basic
writers, 26; feminist
approaches to, 63, 64, 65, 67;
in nineteenth century, 8–9;
twentieth century, 11–12. *See
also* Multicultural classrooms
Writing models, androcentric,
64

Z

Zimmerman, Don H., 59, 60,
61, 68

336740

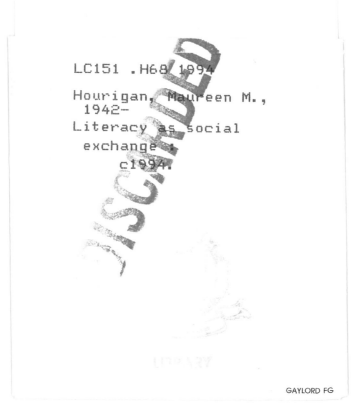